SO-CFE-950

DOWNTOWN TORONTO NEIGHBORHOODS

Washington-Huron-Sussex

Bloor street

Yonge Street

University

Don Vale

South of St. James Town

kensington and the market

Don Valley

Regent Park

Parliament st.

City Hall

Cornwall-Oak

Trefann

Queen street

Wilkins-Berkeley

Front street

Docks

Island

Mcfanwy Phillips

The Real World of City Politics

The Real World of City Politics

by James Lorimer
foreword by Jane Jacobs

**James Lewis & Samuel, Toronto
1970**

Copyright © 1970 by James Lewis & Samuel

ISBN 0-88862-003-9 (cloth)
ISBN 0-88862-004-7 (paper)

Cover design: Christer Themptander

James Lewis & Samuel, Publishers

Printed in Canada

6 5 4 73 74 75

Table of Contents

Acknowledgements

I would like to acknowledge the assistance and encouragement which I have had from many people, in the course of writing the articles, which appeared originally in the *Globe and Mail*, and in preparing this book; in particular Stan Benjamin, Fran Chadwick, Barbara Dawson, Richard Doyle, Edna Dixon, Wolfe Erlichman, Noreen Gaudette, Doreen Govereau, Eleanor Guerin, Sarah Hayward, Julie La Pointe, Mary Murdoch, Dave McKee, Dave Pinkus, Judy Ramsay, Alan Schwam, John Sewell, Marie Smith, Phyllis Tomlinson, Kenny Wright.

All but one of the newspaper articles reprinted here originally appeared in slightly different form in the *Globe and Mail*. "What the people thought of the Cornwall-Oak school site" appeared originally in the *Toronto Star*.

Foreword

Toronto is still a calm and orderly city as cities go. Paradoxically, for that very reason, this book about a half-dozen Toronto civic battles tells us more about the genesis of modern city social disorder and of just how these great settlements become ungovernable than we are apt to find in torrents of reports on cities in advanced stages of demoralization.

By the time a city has become distraught or riotous, it seems obvious to those who govern it that the population is out of control or is becoming so. Measures to meet this crisis — whether they are repressive, placating or both — are intended to bring the governed back under control.

But to the governed, things can look different from this. Long before their anger or demoralization has built to crisis proportions, they have been making a judgment of their own: that government is out of control. It is a judgment that invariably, I think, precedes the *belated* awareness of crisis among those who govern great cities. James Lorimer's reports are of more than local interest and value because they show, quite unblurred by popular disorder, the patterns and policies of a city government becoming incapable of governing a modern city.

What does this mean: a city government getting out of control? Mr. Lorimer shows us in precise and minute detail, almost as if the phenomenon were laid out for us under a microscope. The minute, concrete detail is of the essence: the "experts" making an ill-informed and incompetent decision, to the harm of the neighborhood involved. The crucial missed opportunity for a local improvement, unapparent (or unimportant?) to those same experts. The puppet organizations cultivated by City Hall for playing against citizens' own independent organizations. The law flouted and broken by an organ of government itself. The promises of "citizen participation," and the proof, in events that follow, that the promises were insincere. The slippery unaccountability of decision makers. The jargon intended to deceive. The tenderness with which government treats land speculators or developers; the harshness accorded modest householders. And much, much more; the whole dismal pattern is here, in microcosm. Not least important, we are shown these tricks, meannesses and incompetences being applied where they are always applied first: in the poorest and most helpless parts of the city. The other parts get theirs, later.

There are shockers in this book. One learns how vandals of houses can be wonderfully convenient to a government agency that is seeking to dispossess stubborn householders from a site expropriated for clearance. That is now such a common form of symbiosis in North American cities it has lost its shock value, but here the horror comes through new and clear again — probably because the vandals are children, the agency in question happens to be the Board of Education, and the massive vandalism occurs where such events are reported to have been previously unknown. There is comedy too: we are privy to the embarrassing rationalizations of aldermen trying, unsuccessfully as it turns out (which is why we can see it as comedy), to gerrymander the city wards.

It may seem to some readers that here and there Mr.

Lorimer is somewhat too skeptical about the motives of those who govern. But my own vice in such matters is over-optimism, and in any case Mr. Lorimer is reflecting the already deep disillusionment of the neighborhoods concerned. This is an important part of the whole phenomenon, too: the governed lose trust in the future intents of government because in the past their trust has been betrayed.

At the same time as we scrutinize the malady, the outlines of a remedy reveal themselves. The governments of large, modern cities are not only incomprehensibly complex today, but also their direct effects on citizens' lives are now so ubiquitous that they cannot help but fail when their functions are centrally organized. Many functions must be decentralized and brought under direct, continuing control of local communities within the city. This is a great and unsolved institutional problem of our time, about which there is much talk but no effective progress.

Not many North American cities, if indeed any, have had the benefit of such acute and specific reporting as Mr. Lorimer's at so relatively early a stage in the government's incapacity to govern. There is thus a chance that the insights of his reports can be put to use and help avert eventual crisis. We shall see. Failing that, he has at least given us an instructive and engrossing account of city government in the very act of getting out of control — while citizens are still maintaining their order.

–J.J.
Toronto
January 1970

The Real World of City Politics

Introduction

In late 1966 I moved into the area east of Parliament Street in downtown Toronto. As it happened, late 1966 was the time that Toronto's city planners showed residents of that area detailed plans for an urban renewal scheme. The plan was for a new kind of urban renewal; instead of expropriating all the houses in the area, only some were to be torn down. The others, the houses which were not "too far gone," were to be left in the hands of the people who had always owned them. These people were to be "encouraged" to make substantial renovations and to rehabilitate their properties.

A few residents of the area (which the planners had named "Don Vale") were sufficiently angry and frightened by the prospect of urban renewal and expropriation that they called public meetings and set up a local residents' association. I went to the first meetings out of curiosity, but I soon found myself involved in the political activities of the area. There was an enormous protracted struggle concerning urban renewal in Toronto in 1967-69, and as one of the dozen or so residents on the executive of the Don Vale residents' association I learned about city planning and city planners, urban renewal, the practice of government bureaucracies, and city politics through our experience trying to beat off the city and its plan, trying to create a situation where the residents of the area east of Parliament could themselves plan for their neighborhood. During this period I was gathering material for a book about the people who live in Don Vale, and occasionally I took my tape recorder to the meetings where urban renewal matters were being discussed. Some of the material I assembled I used in the first draft of a book about some of the residents of the Don Vale area, which I expect to be published as *Working People*.

In early 1969 I decided to try writing some newspaper articles on issues which concerned people in the residents' association and others active in similar groups in downtown Toronto. I used transcripts made from my tape recordings and relied heavily on what people themselves actually said about what they thought, and why they held those views. This method proved to work very well as a means of conveying information and expressing the viewpoints of those challenging official decisions and official opinions of city government. Using this technique I wrote weekly articles for the next six months in the *Globe and Mail* on several major political issues: urban renewal, the schools, redevelopment by private and public developers, public housing. As well as worrying a considerable number of people, these subjects also had in common the fact that they had been made public issues by political organizations of downtown, mostly working-class, people who were dissatisfied with the performance of the bureaucracy and the politicians.

For this small book, I chose to include most but not all of the articles printed in the *Globe* series. I have made chapters out of the articles which deal with each major issue. Chapter introductions and connections between articles have been written for this book and are intended to provide the necessary background information and to fill in events which occurred between the times the articles were written. There have been minor editing changes made, and occasionally repetitive or irrelevant material has been deleted. Otherwise the articles are printed here as they appeared originally, though without the photographs which accompanied most of them and with my own title rather than the *Globe's*.

However well these articles may be judged to have conveyed the realities of city politics at some later time when the issues they deal with are dead and all but forgotten, at the time they were published those issues were still contentious, and politicians and officials were obliged to decide what they were going to do. These people reacted uniformly — and violently — to many of the articles. From the first publication on, there was a never-ending stream of complaints from politicians. Once or twice, they found an error on a matter of fact. Generally, though, they didn't complain about inaccuracies, and found it difficult to object that their point of view was not being recorded. Their main complaint was simply that it was wrong, damaging, destructive, and unhealthy for a responsible city newspaper to print this kind of comment on city politics.

Why it should seem illegitimate to the politicians is, I think, explained by the implications of the way the articles were written. Politicians (and employees of city government too) consider themselves to be rather special. They are the authorities; they are the people who have the benefit of full information and expert advice; they are the people who understand the issues which city governments face; and they are the people who have been chosen to make wise decisions. They objected to these articles because their actions and their public statements were not reported with the usual deference, while at the same time those of ordinary citizens were given at least equal weight. In the way newspapers usually write about city politics, there is a constant, perhaps unconscious, deference to these authorities and to the official point of view. This is reflected, for instance, in whom the newspapers quote and pay attention to; if they are writing about the expropriation of 51 houses, they report what the chairman of the

Board of Education and the officials in charge of site acquisition say about why the expropriation is necessary and desirable, automatically deferring to the official explanation and preferring it to counter-explanations of unofficial critics. This deference is also reflected in how the newspapers describe the actions of city government; if they are reporting on what City Council did, they quote the politicians' public relations description of their action and leave it at that. This they do even though newspaper reporters undoubtedly are the best-informed group of people about the realities which lie behind the public relations accounts they report so carefully.

Not only is the view of city government which is provided by the case studies of these chapters not the view usually reflected in newspapers, it is also quite far from that of academic commentators who have written about politics and urban government.

There is in fact an enormous gap between city politics as it exists in the work of academic political theorists and researchers and city politics as it is encountered in real life by ordinary citizens. Take for example, *Urban Political Systems*, a solid and very respectable academic study of metropolitan government in Toronto by Harold Kaplan. Metro Toronto is a different level of city government than the City Council which figures in this book. But many of the city's politicians have been active in Metro politics and there is not much difference in the way the two levels of government function. I remember as I went through the book wondering whether this was the same city, the same kind of city government, that we in Don Vale had encountered. Much of what Kaplan reports about Metro Toronto is interesting; some of his findings, for example on the relation between the views of special interest groups and the major decisions of Metro Toronto Council are very revealing. Nevertheless the world of city politics becomes, in this kind of analysis, rather a dull, benign place. The implicit assumption is that real decisions are made when a vote is taken in the council chamber, and that the significance of particular decisions is expressed by their bland official labels, like expressway extension, urban renewal, or an attempted takeover of the transit authority. It is only when one begins to look carefully at what is involved in an urban renewal project: the costs, benefits, impact on bureaucrats and their powers, effects on local people, and so on, that it is possible to begin to understand what was done and the motives and interests which lay behind the actions of the people involved. The same is true of every other aspect of city government and of urban policy programs. Accounts which rely on official self-description and information from the administration are incomplete and tend to mislead because of what they leave out.

This small book confines itself to reporting what is going on in city politics by discussing a number of specific cases in detail. Because the cases were instances where citizens had publicly challenged or protested what was happening to them, the book is in fact a series of reports from the battlefront. It describes a small number of city government actions and reports on what the city politicians and the citizens said and did on these matters.

I have made no attempt here to propose an analysis of city government which would explain why things work the way they do. It does seem, however, that some new explanations are needed because conventional theories do not explain — do not predict — the actions and decisions which are being produced by real city governments. The problem is too complex to be dealt with properly here; it is a subject I propose to discuss in a later book.

This book concentrates on reporting what is happening in city politics and makes no proposals for reform. There is certainly no doubt that a government which acts in the ways documented in the chapters of this book and which is almost completely invulnerable to pressure, influence, control or real participation by citizens, is in need of great change. Many people are full of ideas about what should be done, but most of them seem to be unaware of how in fact city governments work. The people who have gone through the experiences documented here, and people like them, are now developing proposals for changes, proposals which reflect both an understanding of what is happening now and what it is that citizens need done by a new kind of city government. Their kind of experience and their knowledge of what is really going on are essential in order to have useful ideas about what changes should be made in city government. By helping to share their experience, this book may help create a greater receptiveness to proposals for change in city government and at the same time make people better able to judge what kinds of changes are needed. But the book itself does not explore these possibilities; it sticks to the simple task of reporting. It attempts to record what happened on six or eight issues of great importance to people living in central Toronto in a six-month period in 1969.

Chapter One

Real Political Decision-Making:
The Case of the Cornwall-Oak School Site

When Toronto's Board of Education made up its mind in late 1968 to expropriate 51 houses for a new school just east of the Regent Park public housing project, there was no reason for the trustees or the board's officials to think that this was anything but an ordinary political decision — the kind of thing the board does ten or twenty times every year. No doubt all the usual procedures were followed, and the choice of a site for the school should have been no better and no worse than other expropriation decisions. At secret board meetings officials reported on studies of the alternatives available and made their recommendation: the school should be built on the Cornwall-Oak site. Writing about this decision-making process, Trustee Alan Archer later said: "Officials of the board, following a long and careful study, said there was no practical alternative. We have to provide a school! What better reason can one have? " That was the best explanation Archer and the other trustees produced for their choice.

In the normal course of events, only officials and perhaps politicians would have had access to all the information about the alternatives open to the board.

Outsiders would have had very few facts, and if the site chosen by the board seemed stupid to them, they would nevertheless have been told by politicians that expert officials had considered everything and had made a wise recommendation, which the board was only too happy to follow.

Whatever information the Board of Education had before its decision to expropriate the Cornwall-Oak site, it had no idea of the views of people to be served by the new school or of those living in the houses to be torn down. Not only were none of the people affected consulted; the board was careful to keep the whole thing secret until after the 51 houses had been expropriated and the land was legally owned by the board.

Understandably, the families who were expropriated were unhappy. They voiced their complaints to board officials and to their ward trustees. The trustee who concerned himself with the south part of the ward, Alan Archer, did his best to persuade the expropriated residents to give up and leave quietly. They didn't. Instead, they contacted active members of the residents' associations in the nearby Don Vale and Trefann Court areas and asked lawyer and community organizer John Sewell to help them try to persuade the board to change its mind, and to treat them fairly.

It was the series of public meetings and protests organized by Cornwall-Oak residents and people in surrounding areas whose kids might go to the new school which dragged out into the open a good deal of information about the board's decision and the alternatives before it when it chose the Cornwall-Oak site. As more information became public, greater pressure was put on the board to reverse what was obviously a silly choice. In the controversy about Cornwall-Oak, the way political decision-making really worked in what looked like an ordinary site purchase became clear. It also became clear that the less people know about what the politicians and their bureaucrats are doing, the safer the politicians are.

When Cornwall-Oak residents began to receive compensation offers which they considered unfairly low they decided that they would have to protest what was happening to them. At a public meeting the two ward trustees were invited to explain why the Cornwall-Oak site had been chosen for the school and basis on which the board was making its expropriation compensation offers. The article I wrote on this meeting was published in the *Toronto Star*.

April 23, 1969

**What the people thought
of the Cornwall-Oak school site**

It's a lousy place to build a school — everyone whose kids might go there is agreed about that. The site in question is east of the Regent Park North public housing project, between some recently-built garages owned by the city and a new high-rise apartment now under construction. All the students of the primary school proposed for this site would have to cross one wide busy street — River Street — and some might have to cross Gerrard or Dundas Streets as well.

About 18 months ago, Toronto's city planners reported that the site would not be suitable for new public housing because of traffic and commercial-industrial surroundings. If it's not good enough for houses, residents argue, it's not good enough for a school.

Just as important, a new school could provide at least some of the community and recreational facilities that are so badly needed in Regent Park. Locating it on the wrong edge of the community means that its potential usefulness is minimized.

The other problem about this location is that there are 51 houses now standing where the school is supposed to go. The board passed over at least two vacant sites to expropriate these homeowners.

The reason the board has been forced to reconsider its decision is that people whose homes are being taken or whose kids will be using the school met their school trustees last Monday night in Spruce Court School and said what they thought about the site and the board's compensation offers. The Ward Two trustees, Alan Archer and Maurice Lister, already had heard expropriated homeowners' objections to the board's prices, but the only views they'd heard on the site itself were those of board officials.

Regent Park, Trefann Court, and Don Vale, the areas the school would serve, are Alan Archer's territory. It's on Gerrard Street that he had his barber-shop when he was first elected to the school board. Lister, the university professor, the Doctor of Philosophy, the man in the gray suit with the touch of a British accent, kept well in the background at last Monday's meeting.

Archer arrived a half-hour late. He came in when Lister was being questioned closely about the prices board officials are offering for some of the expropriated homes, and listened for a while before he interrupted to answer a question.

He was soon pinned down to admitting that he had supported the Cornwall-Oak site, though he said he did so reluctantly and only because board officials said there was no practical alternative. That answer didn't satisfy anyone. "Suppose we found a better site? " he was asked. "Would the board back down at that point? "

"Oh, I think it's a little late now," was his answer.

The houses which have been expropriated stand right next to a tract of land which was vacant for some time before work began on the high-rise apartment now going up. "Why do you have to take houses? " one resident asked. "Why didn't you take the vacant lot? "

We would have to pay too much for it, Archer answered, not explaining why vacant land should cost more than land with houses on it. After all the Board of Education can expropriate developers as well as homeowners.

Norm Macdonald, president of the Property Owners' Association in Don Vale, the area just to the north of Regent Park, pressed this point home. "You are cutting off people's homes and lives because a piece of land is too expensive. The question that's in the back of my mind is, who owns the land? Is this vested interests that you're afraid to fight, that you would rather fight homeowners, ordinary working people?"

The people were on the attack, and Archer was backtracking as fast as he decently could. "The Cornwall-River area was not a set thing until just a very short while ago," he said a few minutes later, "I mean we were looking at it, certainly, but it didn't go to the board until January [1969]." That was a rather peculiar thing to say, since the expropriation itself took place in November 1968 just before the new expropriation act took effect.

Members of the Trefann Court residents' group at the meeting pointed out that there are other places where the school could be built, sites which would be safer and better for kids and where homes would not have to be torn down. One of these is in Regent Park itself on a site where a year ago the Toronto Housing Authority wanted to build a new 12-storey apartment building. Another is land where there's now a gas station, a cinema, and a large vacant lot.

By the middle of the meeting, Archer had forgotten his earlier view that it was too late to do anything about the site and he was warming to the Regent Park alternative. "This is the ideal spot for a school; I'd love to see a school in there because this is where the kids are," he said.

He wasn't allowed to say this without being pinned down to something more specific. "Will you propose," Trefann Court's lawyer John Sewell asked, "at the next board meeting that they build the school there instead of at Cornwall and Oak?"

"Yes, I will," Archer replied. Straightforward, simple, definite — he was committed, even though an hour earlier he'd said it was too late to do anything.

But a new site was not the only alternative people at the meeting had in mind. There are three or four other primary schools in the area; they all have portable class-rooms in their grounds now; and they are all long, low, modern buildings.

As one lady who lives in an expropriated house asked: "Why are they only building schools two floors high? All the apartments go up and up."

Archer answered a question the lady hadn't asked. "Metro will only let us build for our immediate needs; they won't let us build for the future at all," he said.

He wasn't allowed to get away with that. Bert Chapman, vice-president of the Don Vale Association of Homeowners and Residents, made the query specific: "Mr. Archer, why are you always spreading schools all over hell's half-acre, and taking people's homes away from them as you did right here for the Spruce Court School? There were beautiful homes, right here where this place is now. And you spread the darn thing out all on one floor. We're seeing this Board of Education grow like an octopus, of which you are two very good tentacles apparently. You expropriate people's homes, you put them to all sorts of trouble. . ."

And, for the one and only time at that meeting, Alan Archer was pushed as far as he could be pushed. He didn't answer Bert Chapman's question; he counterattacked. "Those are only your statements; they aren't true," he said.

Then he was brought back to the issue of compensation. It had alternated with the question of finding another site throughout the meeting. The people from Cornwall and Oak had arrived early; they sat together in the front two rows; and they took turns questioning Lister and Archer. They quoted prices offered, prices of other houses in the city, and said they couldn't find the same kind of house today for less than $20,000. Archer and Lister both thought homeowners should get "a fair price," and Archer used $20,000 as a "good, round figure" to indicate what he thought a fair price might mean.

At the same time, though, he told residents that the board plans to spend $860,000 acquiring the 51 expropri-

talked about a joint development with participation by the Board of Education. But the owners, according to Mr. Sweetman, turned the board's proposals down. It was in the light of this reaction that board officials recommended the Cornwall-Oak site.*

The board did not enter into discussions with the owners of the 51 houses in the Cornwall-Oak area before it selected that site over the vacant GSW land. Nor did it have to. The board has power to expropriate and, under the provincial legislation in force in 1966, if the board had wanted to take 51 houses for a school there was no way (apart from persuading school trustees to change their minds) that the property owners could stop them. The board's expropriation powers are not, however, limited to homeowners. It can expropriate vacant land in exactly the same way. The board did not need the consent or co-operation of Model Knitting Mills to expropriate all or part of its holdings.

Why did it not do so?

Mr. Archer and Mr. Sweetman have said that the vacant land would have been too expensive. Why they have said this is not clear.

The board has now expropriated roughly 77,000 square feet of land. It estimates it will have to pay $950,000 in compensation, about $12.33 a square foot. This figure probably includes no estimate for the cost of compensating tenants for disturbance damages, something which the board appears to be required to pay.

---

*It was Sweetman who told me in a phone conversation about the joint development proposal. I asked if he meant a school in a high-rise apartment building, and he said yes. After this article appeared, one of the owners of Model Knitting Mills Ltd., Percy Smith, contacted both a Globe news reporter and me and told us that he had never been approached about his land by the Board of Education. Several months later, questioned at a board meeting by a trustee about this statement of Smith's, a board official said that Model Knitting Mills didn't realize that they were being approached by the board because this had been done through a real estate intermediary. How an intermediary could have discussed the possibility of a joint development with Model Knitting Mills which involved a school combined with some kind of residential construction — and at the same time kept from the Smiths the fact that they were really dealing with the Board of Education — has never been explained. Trustees were careful not to get down to such a careful cross-examination in public of their officials.

How much would it have had to pay for the vacant land? In 1964, when the tract was sold by General Steel Wares to Model Knitting Mills, according to the Land Transfer Tax Section of the Ontario Government the consideration accompanying the transfer was $1,250,000. This is roughly $5 a square foot, taking the tract as a whole, a figure which seems reasonable for land in that location with development possibilities five years ago.

No doubt in 1966 the market value of the land would have been somewhat higher than what Model Knitting Mills paid for it, partly because of the general increase in land values and partly because by the end of 1966 high-rise rezoning had been confirmed. Even if it had doubled in value by the end of 1966, this would suggest a price of $10 a square foot.

There was a 1968 conveyance of the lands in question from Model Knitting Mills Ltd. to Samola Apartments Ltd., but an examination of the documents on file in the Land Titles Office and City of Toronto Registry Office reveal a transaction so complex that it is difficult to perform a simple calculation of the market value of the lands in 1968.*

In mid-1966, the board was estimating an acquisition cost for the Cornwall-Oak site "not substantially different" from their current estimate, according to a board official. Perhaps this was $10 a square foot. Certainly at that time the land with its houses would not have cost the board much less. And of course the $10 a square foot for Cornwall-Oak is neither much higher nor much lower than the $10 a square foot market value of the GSW vacant land.

Cost of course, need not have been the only consideration in the minds of board members when they were choosing a site for their school. The board might have decided that it could afford to pay more for vacant land in order to avoid having to tear down homes and reduce the already small supply of moderate-cost housing in Toronto.

---

*After this article appeared, Percy Smith of Model Knitting Mills was quoted by the Globe as saying that the 1968 sale price of the part of the tract which was actually conveyed to Samola was a little more than $10 a square foot.

On the other hand, it might have thought that it would be doing Toronto a favor by expropriating houses which misguided planners might otherwise have saved from demolition in an urban renewal project.

Perhaps the board weighed the trouble and problems which the two different sets of property owners could cause them. It was, after all, only in 1966 that people living south of Bloor Street, in Don Mount and Trefann Court in particular, began objecting strenuously and successfully to government expropriation and urban renewal. Board officials might have thought it simpler and faster to deal with 51 separate and inexperienced homeowners than to face the lawyers for the owners of the General Steel Wares land.

But this is only speculation. The key to understanding the board's decision would seem to be in discovering the source of its conviction that the vacant land would have been far more expensive than houses. Board officials certainly would have known that the entire tract of land, three times the size of the Cornwall-Oak site, sold in 1964 for a price which when averaged out over the entire lot comes to $5 a square foot. They should have known in 1966 the current market value of vacant land with highrise development potential. And surely trustees should have insisted on vacant land being considerably more expensive before they would have approved the expropriation of homes.

In the fall of 1966, funds were included in the 1967 board budget for building a school on the Cornwall-Oak site. The Metro Board of Education deleted this item from the city's budget proposals, but in the fall of 1967 it was again included in the city's 1968 budget. This time the Metro board allowed funds for site acquisition on the understanding that funds for construction would be included in the 1969 budget.

So it was not until January, 1968, that the Board of Education had money in its hands to go out and buy its site. But it was by no means too late for it to change its mind about the Cornwall-Oak expropriation. The vacant land remained vacant, and it was not until April 1968 that an application was made for a building permit for new construction on the site. The permit for an excavation for an apartment building was issued April 29, 1968.

But the board waited, and made its move only in November. At a secret meeting November 14, it passed a bylaw expropriating the 51 homes on the Cornwall-Oak site. Whatever were the facts on which that decision was made, one thing is certain: trustees and officials are wrong when they claim that vacant land would have been far more expensive than houses. The fact is that the price per square foot of the two sites would have been about the same.

* * *

Though it had decided in April 1969 to look again at alternatives to the Cornwall-Oak site, the Board of Education continued to try to persuade homeowners and tenants to settle their expropriation compensation claims and to move out. On May 14, the board's property committee had before it a report from its solicitor on the question of whether tenants in the Cornwall-Oak area should be offered compensation by the board for having to give up their tenancies. The new Ontario Expropriations Act gave the board no option but to pay tenants' moving expenses and some other expenses directly related to the expropriation. What the board committee was deciding was whether it had to pay additional compensation because Cornwall-Oak tenants were not going to be able to continue to rent from their current landlords at their current rent levels.

If the Cornwall-Oak tenants had been middle-class high-rise residents with two-year leases on their apartments, there would have been no dispute. If they had 18 months to go on their lease, if their rent was $175 a month, and if the going rent for their apartment was now $200, the provincial act would have required the board to pay the $25 difference for 18 months — $450 — plus an additional amount reflecting the likelihood that they would have been able to renew their lease at a level below the current market rent.

There was no doubt that all but one or two of the Cornwall-Oak tenants were paying less than they would have to pay if they were to rent equivalent accommodation from another landlord. For some, the difference was $30 or $40. For one or two, it was $70 or $80 a month.

The debate centred around the fact that these tenants had no formal leases with their landlords. Legally, they were month-to-month tenants, and could leave with a month's notice from either side. In practice, however, many of them had lived for years in their homes at rents below what they would have had to pay if they had moved into another equivalent home. And they had every prospect of being able to continue to do so for another five or ten or fifteen years. The decision the board's committee had to make — aided, of course, by learned advice from their solicitor — was whether the wording of the legislation entitled Cornwall-Oak tenants to compensation for rent increases they were to face in view of the 'reasonable prospects of renewal' of their month-to-month tenancies in their Cornwall-Oak homes.

Cornwall-Oak tenants heard that this matter was coming up at the May 14 meeting, and they decided with lawyer John Sewell (who had been working with area residents since January) to present a brief to the committee. They contacted Osgoode Hall law professor Grant Sinclair and asked him to submit his opinion on the matter to the board.

May 19, 1969

Compensation for Cornwall-Oak tenants

For 19 years, Mrs. Mary Murdoch has lived with her husband and kids at 205 Oak Street in a carefully-kept two-storey red brick house. They are paying $65 a month rent, a bit less than the $75 to $100 paid by most of their neighbors. If they had to find another house tomorrow, they'd pay $140 to $200 for a similar house in a similar area.

Though it won't be tomorrow, it will be soon that the Murdochs and the 25 or so other renting families on Oak Street and Cornwall Street east of River will have to find somewhere else to live. Their homes are among the 51 expropriated by the board for a site for a new primary school. Last Wednesday, the Board of Education's property committee discussed the question of what compensation the Cornwall-Oak tenants should be offered. Mrs. Murdoch went to the meeting with Mrs. Dyer, who rents a house on Cornwall.

There's no question that they and most of the other families renting houses in the area stand to lose as a result of the expropriation. They pay low rents, not so much because their landlords are generous but because they have earned them, by proving to be stable residents and by keeping up and improving the houses they live in. It takes several years and a considerable amount of good fortune to develop this kind of arrangement with a landlord.

The 11 trustees on the property committee had asked the board's solicitor, Douglas Gilmore, to write a report about whether the tenants are entitled to compensation under the new expropriations act, and obtain a second opinion on the matter. Mr. Gilmore's report was a bit vague, but didn't seem to hold out much promise. "No more than nominal damages should be paid to each of the tenants," it said. When the subject came up in the meeting, he spelled out to the trustees exactly what kind of money he had in mind:

"In case there's any confusion with respect to the nominal amount — I'm talking about the legal nominal amount, that is to say a token payment of one dollar." Mr. Gilmore's explanation of his position was that virtually all the Cornwall-Oak tenants are on a month-to-month arrangement with their landlords, with no written leases. He said that the outside authority he had consulted, R. B. Robinson, QC, had supported his original opinion that nominal compensation only should be paid.

Maurice Lister, trustee for Ward Two which includes the Cornwall-Oak area, pointed out that the act talks about "any rights to renew the tenancy or the reasonable prospects of renewal." The fact that the average Cornwall-Oak tenant has been there for more than six years, that many have been there for ten to twenty years, indicates that they seem to have very good prospects of expecting to have their tenancies renewed every month for another five or ten years. All this information was set out in a report which the trustees had in front of them. Mr. Lister asked the board's solicitor why "reasonable prospects of renewal" didn't apply in the circumstances.

But the solicitor didn't get a chance to answer. Trustee William Ross jumped in with a quotation from the report of the Law Reform Commission on expropriation. The commission argued that "the mere possibility of a renewal is too speculative a matter to warrant compensation." But Mr. Ross neglected to mention that when the new act got through the Ontario legislature, alongside the old phrase of "any rights to renew the tenancy" was a new phrase which indicated that the commission's recommendation had been rejected. The new act specifically referred to " the reasonable prospects of renewal."

Mr. Ross's timely — and misleading — intervention had the desired effect of combining with the solicitor's report in the minds of the other trustees to give them the firm impression that the legislation did not allow them to pay compensation to tenants in the situation of Mrs. Murdoch and Mrs. Dyer. It led Trustee Ying Hope to speculate that perhaps even a dollar was going too far: "Actually, if we're going to propose a nominal amount, this violates the Expropriations Act right there, whether it's a dollar or one cent. Now are we or are we not bound by the Expropriations Act, as was covered by this clause? If we are, then we can't possibly make a move; we're frozen with it."

Trustee Alex Thompson toyed with the idea of paying more than a dollar. "I think we are committed to not paying any more than we're obliged to, unfortunate as that may be. A nominal amount can be stretched a little but it couldn't be stretched to anything, say, more than $5 and that's a slap in the face too. So I guess we'd better stick to the dollar."

Only Mr. Lister expressed any doubts about this proposal: "My own opinion is that this is not really a fair method of dealing with it; these people have been forced to move by an action on our part, and I feel that the very least we could do would be to deal with their moving costs."

But he received no support, and Mr. Ross was quick to move to end the discussion. Just as he was about to succeed, lawyer John Sewell (who is working with the Cornwall-Oak residents) put a carbon copy of a letter from a law professor at Osgoode Hall in front of Mr. Lister. The letter, written by Professor Grant Sinclair who teaches expropriation law, stated that under the new act the Cornwall-Oak tenants *are* entitled to compensation. It had been sent to the board at Mr. Sewell's request the previous week; but, said the chairman of the property committee, it had never arrived.

Prof. Sinclair was at the meeting, and Mr. Lister was anxious that he be allowed to speak to the committee. Some procedural moves by Mr. Ross almost prevented this, but in the end the other committee members agreed with Mr. Hope that he should be heard "out of courtesy."

Prof. Sinclair did not mince words: "Perhaps I should comment on your solicitor's comments and on the opinions as expressed by Mr. Robinson, QC; with due respect, I suggest to you that under the new legislation they're wrong." He then took the committee on a careful tour of the new Expropriations Act to show exactly how it provides for compensation for month-to-month tenants like most of the Cornwall-Oak families. He pointed out that a "tenant" is defined as any tenant of any kind whatsoever, and "owner" in turn is defined to include tenants. He referred to Section 13 of the act which says that the expropriating authority *shall* pay compensation to all owners (which would include tenants, because of the act's peculiar definition of the term). The same section also says that compensation is to be calculated on the basis of the market value of the expropriated interest in the land, disturbance costs and relocation.

Then he pointed to Section 18, where instructions are given on how to calculate tenants' disturbance costs. The expropriator is directed to look at the length of the tenant's term and the length remaining, both of little importance for month-to-month tenants. But the expropriating authority must also examine "any rights to renew the tenancy or the reasonable prospects of renewal." It is this, the reasonable prospects of renewal, coupled with the facts of the situation where tenants have had monthly terms renewed for an average of more than six years, which provides the main grounds for paying them disturbance damages.

Prof. Sinclair summed up: "My view is that the opinion given to you by your solicitor, with all due respect, as confirmed by Mr. Robinson, with all respect, is clearly wrong under this legislation."

The committee, which had agreed to let Prof. Sinclair speak, had not guaranteed him they would listen to — or even hear — what he had to say. Trustee Hazel MacDonald, the chairman, tried to reassure Prof. Sinclair, Mrs. Murdoch and Mrs. Dyer that they would consider his opinion carefully. "On behalf of the committee, Mr. Sinclair, I would like to thank you and the others who are with you and, uh, believe me we will take this under very deep consideration. So thank you all for coming."

The committee then went into private session to decide what to do, but there was little doubt about what would happen. The next morning, the board's secretary dictated the committee's decision to me on the phone. It was that "no compensation be paid the tenants, and the solicitor write tenants and owners to explain the board's position on the matter."

* * *

The board's "reconsideration" of the Cornwall-Oak site and alternatives to it took from April until September. To cover themselves, board officials finally contacted the owners of the GSW vacant land. They were told they could have the whole parcel or any portion of it that they wanted for about $10 a square foot. That, of course, was the asking price; and no public body with expropriating powers has to pay the asking price for land if the compensation required under the expropriations act is less.

The main part of the "reconsideration" was discussions between the board and the Ontario Housing Corporation about the possibility of building the school on vacant land in Regent Park. While this was going on, board officials were doing their best to make the Cornwall-Oak site a *fait accompli*. They pressured, cajoled, and persuaded tenants and owners to move out. As people left, they arranged for the minimum possible protection for the vacant houses, and kids from surrounding areas took up the board's implicit invitation to spend their summer holidays wrecking the houses. By September, OHC had come up with what appeared to Cornwall-Oak residents and people from surrounding areas as an extremely attractive offer designed to persuade the board to build its school within Regent Park North. As usual, the debate on this new alternative and the decision to pass it up in favor of Cornwall-Oak was made at a secret meeting on the basis of a secret report prepared by board officials. After the decision was made, Trustee Maurice Lister showed me the secret report. It managed to find nothing favorable whatsoever to say about the Regent Park site or any of the alternatives to Cornwall-Oak. To everyone's surprise and astonishment, the board's officials came to the conclusion that they had been right all along.

September 22, 1969

Why they went ahead with the Cornwall-Oak site

Toronto's Board of Education has made an inexcusable blunder in deciding to go ahead with a proposed new school to serve children from Regent Park on the Cornwall-Oak Streets site, across River Street from the housing project, rather than on vacant land within Regent Park which has been offered to the board by Ontario Housing Corporation for $1.

The decision, made ten days ago at a secret meeting, was made public last week not by the board but by the remaining residents of the 51 houses expropriated on the Cornwall-Oak site.

When it made its decision, the board had before it two alternatives. The first was to continue with the expropriated Cornwall-Oak site, for which plans had been prepared. Estimated cost of the land is $950,000; of the building, $1.5 million.

The second was to negotiate with OHC to build the school on a play area within Regent Park North. A study made by OHC architects during the summer showed that the school of the size required by the board could be built on the Regent Park site without crowding the apartment buildings and baseball diamond already there. It would have been a four-storey building with two basements. At an estimated cost of $2.5-million for the building alone, it would have provided the same school facilities plus underground parking and a swimming pool in the basements. In other words, if it had chosen the Regent Park site, the board could have had the same-sized school plus a swimming pool for the same amount of money it was proposing to spend to build on Cornwall-Oak.

There is, however, more than just the cost-free swimming pool to be taken into account; there is first, the issue of safety. All 1,000 children who could attend the Cornwall-Oak school would have to cross River Street four times a day. River Street is a heavily travelled commercial artery. There is little parking, local shopping, or stop-and-go traffic to slow things down. Last year, according to Cornwall-Oak residents, there were at least five injury-producing accidents when the 200 children living on Cornwall, River and Oak were crossing River to go to school. If the Regent Park site were used, most if not all of the children attending the school would not have to cross any streets to get there. School trustees, aware of the potential impact of the charge that they are disregarding children's safety, are now talking about building a bridge over River Street to the Cornwall-Oak site. That would be a far inferior solution to having a location where crossing a street of this kind would be unnecessary.

There is also the question of the new school's neighborhood. In Regent Park, the school would be surrounded by green open space and apartment buildings. On the Cornwall-Oak site, it will have a high-rise apartment and vacant land to the north, a factory to the south and the Don Valley to the east. The valley has several times proved a fatal attraction to children in this area and bringing them to its edge every day to go to school will serve only to put them closer to it. Said one Cornwall-Oak resident at a press conference last Thursday called to protest the board's decision: "There's a railway at the bottom, there's a river at the bottom, there's a highway at the bottom. We know from experience: we see them swimming in the Don. Three or four years ago a kid was killed on the road. There was a couple of little kids cut to pieces on the railroad track."

The board should also have considered the problem of recreation facilities for Regent Park. For years residents and social workers have complained about the lack of space and facilities within the housing project to keep children and teenagers occupied. Last summer, there was a well-publicized march to raise funds for a swimming pool. One of the prominent marchers was the trustee for the ward, Alan Archer. This summer Regent Park mothers were demonstrating and picketing about the swimming pool.

By far the most satisfactory location for facilities of this kind would be within Regent Park. The board certainly has no intention of putting a swimming pool in the Cornwall-Oak site and would do so in Regent Park only because OHC would make that a condition of giving up the land. The new school on the Regent Park site would provide an ideal opportunity to deal with this unquestioned need for recreational facilities. As OHC managing director H. W. Suters commented in a press statement last week: "This could be an outstanding example of two public agencies working together to provide much-needed facilities."

Weighing all the factors involved, there can be no doubt that the new school incorporating community facilities on the Regent Park site would be far superior to what the board has suggested for Cornwall-Oak. Its attractiveness to OHC is indicated by the trouble and expense OHC went to during the summer to develop detailed plans for a school on its land to the board's specifications, after residents' protests forced the board in April to reconsider. If public agencies were not so polite about each other, OHC would probably be extremely bitter about the board's recent decision.

What makes this decision seem more unjustifiable is that the board was in no way limited in choosing between these two sites. A third possible site is a tract of vacant land immediately to the north of Cornwall-Oak and also east of River Street. It has all the same locational disadvantages of the Cornwall-Oak site, but it has the compelling advantage that the board would not have to demolish any houses in order to build its school there.

The fact that they have completely ignored this vacant land should be a source of great embarrassment to trustees. Yet apparently it is not. For a long time, they told anyone who would listen that of course this vacant land would be more expensive than adjoining houses because it had been rezoned to allow high-rise residential redevelopment. In April this year in a newspaper article, for example, ward trustee Alan Archer said: "The site was purchased by a developer for a fantastic price and it would be extremely extravagant and totally irresponsible if the Toronto board tried to compete with private developers. (It was reported that the cost was about $25 a square foot)."

It is now obvious that this is total nonsense. "Fantastic price" turns out to be about $5 a square foot. The figure of $25 a square foot turns out to have no connection whatsoever with the price the land was selling for at the time in 1968 when the board was apparently deciding whom to expropriate. Only a few weeks ago, owners of the land were reported ready to consider selling to the board the 200,000 square feet as yet unbuilt for about $10 a foot. The board estimates it will finally pay between $12 and $13 a square foot for the Cornwall-Oak site. Yet on the phone last week Mr. Archer reiterated to me how expensive this vacant land would be.

Why, in spite of all this, did the board decide to press on with the Cornwall-Oak site? It appears that in fact what happened was that trustees and officials organized things last winter and this spring so that by now they would have no choice but to continue.

This they did in a number of ways. First, they did their best to discourage as firmly as possible local residents who wanted to try to get the board to change its mind. Said Mrs. Arthur Crewe at last Thursday's press conference: "We asked Alan Archer in January, if we stick together could we stop it? And he said, 'No way.' "

This spring and summer, board officials dealt with Cornwall-Oak residents and property owners, persuading them to move and, if possible, to settle with the board. This helped considerably to reduce the number of their most vocal critics. As people moved out, houses were boarded up and two guards were hired for the properties as is required by the city's bylaw. These proved ineffective at stopping children and teenagers from vandalizing houses in the area. "The guards can't do anything," said Mrs. Crewe, "because the kids are stronger than they are and are frightened of nothing." During the summer Cornwall-Oak residents were harassed by these kids who broke into many houses and smashed up their insides. Rubble was thrown out of some and into others.

Said Mrs. Crewe: "One man came back from his holidays and he had no house left. They ripped his furniture to pieces, they tore every mattress, they stole

$85 worth of groceries, his kitchen was absolutely ruined, his children's clothes were all cut and he had what he was standing in. Everything else was gone."

"And the school board didn't help him," added Mrs. George La Pointe, "and it's on account of the school board that it happened. We had none of this before the school board came near here."

The houses have been so badly damaged, residents say, that it would be very expensive to repair them so that they could be lived in again. Slowly but surely, people have been forced out by this harassment, so that now only nine families remain in the 51 houses. These conditions developed partly as a result of actions by board officials, partly because of inaction on the part of trustees who made no strong public objection to what was going on.

In spite of this situation, which had the effect of leaving trustees with little choice when they finally met to consider the Regent Park alternative ten days ago, board officials were careful to reduce to an absolute minimum the outside chance that the trustees might not go ahead with the Cornwall-Oak site. This they did by writing a secret report which managed to find nothing favorable to say about the Regent Park alternative. On the basis of all the criteria these officials could think of, they found the Cornwall-Oak site preferable. They presented their recommendation to the trustees as if the matter were cut and dried.

And of course it was. If trustees had changed their minds and decided to build in Regent Park, they would have been admitting openly that they had made a blunder. By law they would have been required to withdraw their expropriation and to offer the houses they have now purchased back to their former owners at the price the board paid. Yet a summer's neglect has had a disastrous effect on them.

There was and is the risk that Regent Park residents might realize they have lost an opportunity to acquire the recreation centre and swimming pool they have been trying for years to obtain. So far, however, no one in

Regent Park seems to have noticed what has happened. So, instead of admitting to their original mistake, the trustees have compounded it.

* * *

The secret meeting in early September when the board decided to proceed with their school on the Cornwall-Oak site was not the last they heard of the matter. When they learned about it Cornwall-Oak residents called another public meeting, this time in a church in Regent Park, and invited Regent Park residents as well as people from neighboring areas. They also invited board members and asked them to explain their decision to proceed with Cornwall-Oak.

Ward trustee Maurice Lister was there; Alan Archer did not attend. The only other trustee present was William Ross, a former board chairman and one of the more powerful board members. It was he who had managed the debate about tenant compensation at the property committee so well. Ross got up early in the meeting and began to say that he had always favored careful study by the board of alternatives to Cornwall-Oak, and that if a better alternative could be found he would support it. In fact, however, Ross had always been unenthusiastic about reopening the Cornwall-Oak question, and at the May property committee meeting had stated clearly that he felt there was no doubt that the board would never alter its original decision. A Trefann Court resident, Gus Dion, told Ross he was being "careless with the truth." Ross got up and left in a huff.

A few of the people at the meeting were residents of Regent Park, and they began to argue about whether a school within Regent Park North would be desirable. The proposal was denounced by a Regent Park North resident, Bud McCormack, who has long been politically active in the area's businessmen's association and in Conservative politics. It was clear that when McCormack said the people of Regent Park didn't want a school built on what is a rarely-used playground, he was speaking not for the residents of Regent Park but for himself. An attempt was made to persuade McCormack and the other 'representatives' of Regent Park to take a poll of residents to see whether they would be prepared to negotiate about the school with the Board of Education and OHC. They said they would do so, but in fact they did nothing.

Nevertheless a poll of residents was taken by John Sewell and some people from Cornwall-Oak and Regent Park. Questionnaires were distributed and then picked up. Response was about 50 percent and returns showed 80 percent preferring to have the school in Regent Park rather than on the Cornwall-Oak site. The main reason for this preference was not the swimming pool and community facilities which were required by OHC if the school was to be built in Regent Park; rather residents of the project proved to be most worried about the safety of kids crossing River Street regularly.

At the next meeting of the Board of Education, Trustee Maurice Lister moved that the matter be re-opened. The board heard representatives of a number of citizens' groups argue that it should look more closely at the possibility of building the school in Regent Park. It also heard Bud McCormack, speaking, he said, on his own behalf, say that no one in Regent Park wanted the school within the project. Then John Sewell reported the results of his poll.

Before a vote was taken on the motion to re-open the matter, board officials were given a chance via trustees' questions to give their views on some of the issues which had been raised in the public discussion of the Cornwall-Oak expropriation. It was at this meeting that the board official in charge of site acquisition, Harry Facey, said that the cost of the vacant land would be about $13 a square foot whereas the Cornwall-Oak site would cost the board about $10. Facey assumed the board would have to pay the asking price for the land; he assumed that the board would pay no more than its original estimate for expropriation compensation in Cornwall-Oak; and he seemed to base his figures on an erroneous calculation of the size of the expropriated site. Yet no one questioned him on his views; the trustees merely nodded in agreement. They and Facey had been right all along. The motion to re-open the discussion was lost, and a few weeks later the board began tearing down homes on the Cornwall-Oak site.

Chapter Two

Ward Boundaries:
"Making City Politics Safe for Politicians"

The way electoral boundaries are drawn has a lot to do with who can win elections. So there is nothing closer to the hearts of a group of politicians in office than a discussion about how the boundaries of the constituencies they represent should be changed. At the more serious levels of government, the provincial and the federal, the matter has been recognized as something too hot for the political party in power to decide on its own; the question has been handed over to 'independent' commissions who are supposed to be politically neutral and to draw boundaries that are fair and do not give any party an advantage. In city government, however, there is usually only one quasi-party — those who are "in" — which encompasses everyone on city councils. This common interest makes it possible for them to draw their own boundaries. Provincial legislation in Ontario formally gives the Ontario Municipal Board, a semi-judicial body which supervises some of the more important activities of municipal governments, the responsibility for drawing municipal electoral boundaries. In practise, however, councils prepare a map which they submit to the OMB for approval, and the map is very likely to be approved unless formal objections to it are registered with the OMB.

Toronto's City Council got itself into the situation where new electoral boundaries for the city were necessary. It happened when the council voted to do away with its Board of Control, a body of four controllers (plus the mayor) elected in a city-wide vote. The arrangement was that the two controllers polling the highest number of votes plus the mayor sat on the Council of Metropolitan Toronto, a body made up of representatives from the six borough governments which have been united for certain important activities into a city-wide government. Also sitting on Metro Council were the aldermen polling the highest number of votes in each of the city's nine wards. This produced 12 city representatives. With the Board of Control being abolished, however, the city politicians had to devise another way of selecting the city's 12 metro councillors.

A second problem created by the abolition of the Board of Control was that it would leave four empty seats in the council chamber of the new city hall. Not only that: it would reduce by four the number of city politicians who could get elected to office.

City Council decided to deal with these difficulties in the simplest way possible: they decided to re-divide the city into 11 instead of nine wards, each ward electing two aldermen. The alderman in each of the 11 wards polling the most votes would sit on Metro Council, along with the mayor. Two times 11 plus the mayor would equal 23 city politicians, just as two times nine plus four controllers and the mayor had equalled 23. Having made that decision, the council requested the city clerk to prepare a proposal for the boundaries of the 11 new wards.

Though the council gave him no instructions whatever about the criteria he should use in drawing this map, the city clerk certainly had a strong sense of political reality and knew that he was not being asked to prepare a map which would make the task of re-election for the sitting aldermen any more difficult than necessary. His

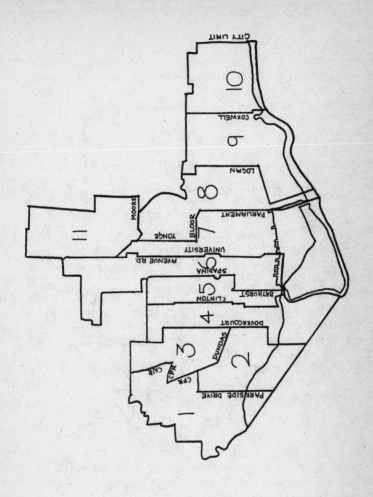

STRIP PLAN
prepared by the City Clerk

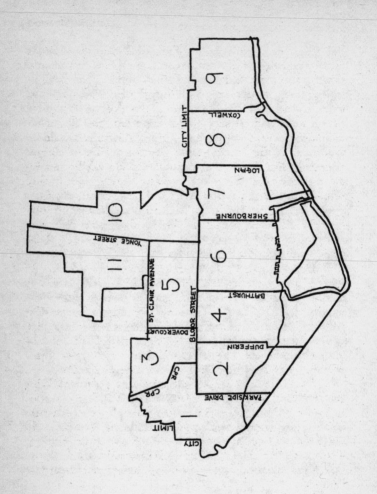

BLOCK PLAN
prepared by the City Clerk

first plan, shown on the accompanying map, had the six outer wards more or less block-shaped; the five central wards were long, irregularly-shaped strips. This map became known as the city clerk's strip plan. The strip plan created wards with *as few new voters as possible* for the sitting aldermen. By using this criterion, the city clerk maximized the chances that sitting aldermen would be re-elected in the coming civic elections. This is because experience has shown that incumbents in a ward generally are re-elected no matter how good or bad they are. If they were forced to run in unfamiliar territory, sitting aldermen would be deprived of this important advantage. Unfortunately, though the city clerk's strip plan met this criterion of the aldermen, it did not meet some of the more commonly used criteria for electoral boundaries.

The city clerk's proposal continued the practice of joining upper-middle-class areas north of Bloor Street in central Toronto, Forest Hill, and Rosedale, with low-income working-class areas south of Bloor Street. The practical effect of this arrangement has always been that people from north of Bloor Street control whatever constituency political organizations exist; and these often provide the crucial votes which determine an election.

When the city clerk's proposal was published, both the residents' association in Don Vale and the organization in Trefann Court, areas which had been placed in the same ward as upper-class and upper-middle-class Rosedale, decided that the proposal for their ward was unsatisfactory. They voted to send representatives armed with briefs to object when the matter came up before the Board of Control.

But the Board of Control was not at all anxious to hear citizens' views on the city clerk's map. The day the matter came up for discussion, the board heard first from three or four aldermen who wanted a few small adjustments made here and there in the city clerk's plan. Then there was a move to send the plan, with these changes, to City Council for approval without hearing any citizens on the matter.

Both Trefann and Don Vale groups had submitted their written briefs by the deadline required for them to speak at that board meeting. The board's rules are that any group which follows these procedures can address the board on any matter whatsoever. When it was apparent that the controllers were hoping to avoid hearing from Trefann and Don Vale, John Sewell and I (as the representatives for that day's debate from the two groups) got up and objected. Sewell read the board its rules of procedure. The controllers did not relent, but they decided to have a special meeting of City Council at which all citizens' groups would be invited to present briefs. In addition, Controller Margaret Campbell successfully moved that the city clerk make public all the alternative maps which he had prepared, including a map dividing the city in 11 more or less block-shaped wards.

At that special council meeting briefs were presented by a number of citizens' groups — businessmen's associations, residents' groups, and municipal political parties. Most of these argued that by the criteria of electoral boundary-drawing the city clerk's block plan was far more satisfactory than the strip plan he had recommended. After the briefs were read, the council debated the issue and made its decision.

May 5, 1969

The politicians decide their ward boundaries

It was a week ago today that the members of Toronto City Council were trying to explain to the 76,000 people who live in central Toronto south of Bloor Street why they can't be trusted to have wards and aldermen of their own. What made this rather embarrassing for the large majority of council members who were determined not to change the long contorted strip boundaries in the map recommended by the city clerk for the three central wards was that an angel choir of four of their number (Controller Margaret Campbell, and Aldermen Charles Caccia, Tony

O'Donohue and — much to everyone's surprise — Michael Grayson) was virtuously pointing out that the politicians were doing this for the good of themselves, not for the people of the city.

The Trefann Court and Don Vale Residents' Associations submitted briefs asking for compact block wards in the centre of the city to complement those the city clerk had proposed for the west, east and north ends.

The problem for the majority of council members who wanted to support the city clerk's map was to think of some plausible reasons for doing so. The mayor, William Dennison, Controllers June Marks and Fred Beavis, and Aldermen David Rotenberg, Mary Temple and Ben Grys all had their turn. But they kept stumbling all over themselves in their arguments, and several times demonstrated why it is in fact unfair and harmful to Trefann, Don Vale, Regent Park and other central city areas to draw ward boundaries the way the clerk proposed. The angel choir refrained from saying this directly, but insisted on pointing out the naked aldermanic self-interest which was being clothed by the elaborate debate.

Mrs. Marks was the only council member who justified the city clerk's central wards on the basis of their entertainment value for aldermen. "I as a representative of Ward Two feel that I'm probably as justified as anybody to assure you that by having this mixture and by representing this mixture in one ward, it is the most *interesting* ward to represent, if this is any consolation to you . . ."

Charles Cacccia: *"This also becomes a job which would defeat the greatest statesman."*

David Rotenberg talked about homogeneity. "The question really then becomes whether the persons on this council should represent a homogeneous group of people or a number of groups of people," he said. A few minutes later he added: "Quite frankly, Mr. Chairman, I think I can better represent the entire citizens of Toronto on this council by having a heterogeneous ward to represent rather than a homogeneous block." By saying this, though, Mr. Rotenberg was agreeing with the people of Trefann and

Don Vale in spite of himself. He was implying that aldermen from the east, the west and the north go to council to represent their wards which are more or less homogeneous. Aldermen from the central city wards, however, represent not their wards but "the entire citizens of Toronto." This is another way of saying that they do whatever they think they should, since their constituents are generally divided among themselves on many important issues.

Tony O'Donohue: *"I think that when a politician draws lines he has his own interests first, there's no doubt about that."*

The mayor talked about not making the job too easy for aldermen. "When the question comes up, is this going to be easier for aldermen or controllers or anyone representing these people, is it going to be easier for them if it's a strip ward with the haves in the north and the have-nots in the south . . . is it going to be easier to represent that kind of ward? And I guess the answer is, no, it isn't going to be as easy to represent that kind of a ward as it would be if you had a ward where everybody was in one camp or the other and you could speak out strongly and boldly."

This is just what the Trefann and Don Vale groups had said that they want and don't now have: representatives who can speak strongly and boldly for the people of their areas. In the mayor's mind strong representation (which he didn't object to for the people who live in the east end of the city or the west end) suddenly became bad when it's for Trefann and Regent Park. He found himself calling it anti-democratic — with block wards "it might even be possible to get along without the meetings being held" — and irresponsible — "you would be in a position where you didn't have the responsibility on your shoulders."

Margaret Campbell: *"How we can sit here and play politics with this situation I don't know, and yet in effect this is what each of us is doing in one way or another."*

Mary Temple supported strip wards in the central city on the grounds that they would provide an educational experience for the aldermen who, she said, should know the problems of the upper brackets and the lower brackets both. Unfortunately, however, she made this statement immediately after explaining why it is better for constituents in a part of the city she is directly concerned with to have wards which encompass similar interests and problems. This came up when she was explaining her support for having the Parkside-Roncesvalles strip joined to the ward which includes the Parkdale area. "It is a logical inclusion in the Parkdale area," she said. "The problems which affect the Parkdale area affect these people and they are divorced from the Swansea area and the area north, their interests are tied up with the interests of the Parkdale area." It was exactly the same argument which Trefann and Don Vale had used to explain why their ward should include the 20,000 people living on the other side of Parliament Street rather than the 20,000 residents of Rosedale. In that case, however, Mrs. Temple apparently felt that the interests of these people could and should be sacrificed to the aldermen's need for education in the problems of life.

Michael Grayson: *"There's more at stake here than jobs."*

The unreality of all the fancy arguments trotted out at the meeting for strip wards joining Rosedale with Regent Park was suddenly, and no doubt unconsciously, revealed near the end of the meeting by Alderman Helen Johnston, who now represents those two areas. She was explaining the small "adjustments" she wanted made to the middle of the three proposed central-city strip wards, and she was asked if she had consulted residents of her ward before deciding on her position. "May I say," she replied, "that I have been talking to North Rosedale, South Rosedale Ratepayers and also Summerhill Ratepayers' Association, and they were all in accord — they were not too concerned with which way the boundaries went."

Mrs. Johnston has the advantage of several years of education in the problems of "upper brackets and lower brackets." She's had the "responsibility" of having to settle in her own mind disagreements between different groups in her ward. In practice, however, when it comes to a question Rosedale doesn't much care about, but which Trefann and Don Vale are up in arms over, Mrs. Johnston decided on her position after consultations which *did not go south of Bloor Street*. This is the practical reality of strip wards in the central city, of heterogeneous populations, of different interests and problems. Someone gets ignored, and it's usually Regent Park, Trefann Court and Don Vale.

The debate was, of course, window-dressing. All but four of the 23 council members had gone to the meeting ready to approve the city clerk's strip plan. Briefs and delegations made no difference to them, nor did the arguments of their colleagues. Their personal interest in re-election came first, and the city clerk's strip map was approved because it was the best guarantee available that they would all be safely re-elected in familiar wards in the next election.

* * *

When Ron Haggart, writing about this debate in the Toronto *Telegram*, summed up what had happened, he called it "making city politics safe for the aldermen." That was, of course, exactly what went on.

Two months later, the city's proposed map was up for discussion at a public hearing of the Ontario Municipal Board. The board, a provincial body set up to supervise municipalities, operates very much like a court. The municipality sends one of its lawyers and makes a case for whatever it wants to do by calling witnesses who testify under oath. Individuals or groups who oppose the proposal can present briefs to the board, or they can hire lawyers to represent them. Their lawyers can cross-examine the municipality's witnesses and call their own witnesses. It is a setting which makes impossible the normal burblings of politicians like those that occurred at the city council meeting on ward boundaries.

Trefann Court sent John Sewell as its lawyer to the OMB hearing. Sewell called a number of witnesses, some outsiders, some residents and people working in the ward. Don Vale hired a prominent lawyer, Robert Montgomery, who agreed to present their case for a reduced fee. About a dozen other groups presented briefs, all but one of which argued that the OMB should throw out the strip plan recommended by Toronto's City Council and adopt instead the block plan the city clerk had drawn up.

The first half-hour or so of the day-long hearing was absolutely incredible to the people who had been fighting the obviously-lost battle with City Council on the issue. Before the city's lawyer was seriously launched into his case, the chairman of the OMB, J.A. Kennedy, was asking the city's only witness, the city clerk, questions which showed that Kennedy knew what the fight was about and that he wasn't particularly well-disposed to the strip plan.

Following the hearing, there were outraged screams from city politicians who objected to Kennedy's treatment of the city's witnesses and the city's plan. They accused him of being rude and unfair; what they were really trying to do was make it clear that they'd make life difficult for him if he rejected the strip plan. I wrote a summary of what actually happened at the hearing. I had neither a tape nor a transcript of the hearing; the quotations are not in quotation marks because I was not certain that they were absolutely accurate, but they convey quite closely what was said.

July 7, 1969

The strip plan has its day in court

The city was represented at the hearing on ward boundaries by its senior counsel, Michael Fram, and Mr. Fram called one witness only, City Clerk Edgar Norris.

Following the instructions of City Council, Mr. Fram and Mr. Norris put before the OMB four alternative proposals: the strip plan (which Council had approved), two minor variations on the strip plan, and the block plan. All four had been prepared by the city clerk's department. The city recommended to the OMB that it adopt the original strip plan.

Mr. Norris was evidently nervous about the existence of the block plan, and in his testimony tried to explain it away as a rather trivial experiment. It had, he said, been drawn up three years ago when someone at City Hall was wondering whether it was possible to divide the city into 11 wards. The block plan was nothing more than an exercise to show that this was possible. Its authors had paid attention to no principles of constituency boundary drawing, said Mr. Norris, except that they wanted 11 wards and they wanted the number of people in those wards to be as equal as possible.

What other considerations besides population, asked Mr. Kennedy at this point, should be taken into account?

Mr. Norris seemed taken aback by the question. "I'll be guided by the experts," he said. But Mr. Fram had just led Mr. Norris through testimony about his many years in the city clerk's department, his experience with civic elections and his service on electoral boundary advisory bodies in order to establish his *own* claim to expertise.

Mr. Fram then began leading Mr. Norris through the boundaries of each of the 11 wards on the strip plan. When they got to Ward Four, bounded by Dovercourt on the west and Christie-Clinton on the east, Mr. Kennedy stopped him.

How wide is that ward? Mr. Kennedy asked.

About a mile, said Mr. Norris.

How long is it?

Maybe two and a half miles, Mr. Norris replied.

But it was obvious from the map that the ward was much more than two-and-a-half times as long as it is wide. A moment later, Mr. Norris altered his opinion to say that it was closer to two-thirds of a mile wide.

Then Mr. Norris counterattacked, not something a witness under oath generally does. Are you interested in old boundaries, Mr. Chairman? he asked Mr. Kennedy.

At this point Mr. Kennedy became very impatient. I'm interested in people, he replied. I'm not interested in old boundaries. I want to know how long it takes to walk from one end of the ward to the other. There seem to be some people at City Hall who think that no matter how thin you slice them, they're still wards. I'm concerned with the populations of these wards and with the communities.

Mr. Kennedy then turned to Mr. Norris. What's wrong specifically with the block plan? he asked.

I don't know that it provides for retaining communities, Mr. Norris replied. I would have to ask the Planning Board about that. But I don't see anything wrong with any of the plans.

There must be something wrong with the block plan, Mr. Kennedy insisted. There must be some reason why you did not recommend it and City Council did not adopt it. What do you know to be wrong with the block plan? he asked Mr. Norris again.

I haven't examined it, Mr. Chairman, said Mr. Norris.

But you prepared it, Mr. Kennedy said in exasperation.

That was not quite the end of Mr. Norris's testimony, but when he was finished on the stand the city had established no case for its proposal, and its opponents had not yet said a word.

Two organizations were represented by lawyers at the hearing, and presented cases supported by witnesses in favor of the block plan and opposing the strip plan.

One of these was the Trefann Court Residents' Association, represented by John Sewell. Mr. Sewell called Norman Thomas, minister of WoodGreen Church, who talked about the community around his church and its concerns. Ian Burton, a geographer at the University of Toronto, explained why communities generally have compact, simple shapes and boundaries.

The Trefann association's third witness was Jane Jacobs, an author who has a wide reputation for her carefully-observed and sensible ideas about what constitutes a neighborhood in a large city, how neighborhoods work, how they take care of themselves and how they provide a strongly-felt geographical identity for people who live in large cities. She said that she thought one of the serious weaknesses of the strip plan was the way it would tend to discourage neighborhood and community activities. Strip wards make it easy for people living in the south end, like the residents of Trefann and Regent Park, to blame the people at the north end of the ward for their problems. It provides them with an excuse for not trying to get their problems solved.

The lawyer for the Don Vale association, Robert Montgomery, called two more witnesses. The first, Ernest Lilienstein, a sociologist at York University, explained that urban communities are usually relatively homogeneous and contain people with similar (though by no means identical) ethnic backgrounds, incomes and occupations.

Mr. Montgomery's other witness was Terry Fowler, a professor of political science at York. Mr. Fowler has done specialized research work on constituency boundaries and methods of electing municipal representatives in Canada and the United States. Mr. Fowler pointed out that the logic of geographical wards within a larger jurisdiction is to allow local areas, neighborhoods and communities to have their interests and concerns represented. The alternative is to have elected representatives chosen in very large wards with several representatives each, or to have at-large elections for the city as a whole. He said that his research has shown that municipal governments with representatives elected at large or from big wards are not as good at developing policies and at responding to the interests of people as municipal governments with small wards that allow for strong representation of the communities and neighborhoods within the city.

Mr. Fram concentrated his attack on Mr. Fowler's detailed local knowledge of Toronto. He told Mr. Fowler that what he had done was to take a good piece of political theory and to apply it to Toronto without knowing anything about the city.

He pressed Mr. Fowler hard. Your idea is to divide up

the city into communities, he said, using geographical and cultural boundaries. Don't you pay attention to history?

You look at the history of common ties and common interests, Mr. Fowler replied.

Don't you really want to divide the city up into lower-, middle- and upper-income groups? Mr. Fram asked.

It's hard to generalize, Mr. Fowler replied. The only thing that's clear is that you would be separating the very high from the very low incomes.

Do I take it, Mr. Fram continued, that you think that municipal politics should be a class confrontation?

Would that be in addition to or as a substitute for the confrontation that now occurs at City Hall? Mr. Fowler said.

I'm talking about class war, Mr. Fram said. You are insisting that Rosedale and Trefann Court should have different representatives.

I wouldn't describe that as a call to the barricades, Mr. Fowler replied.

As well as these two cases argued by lawyers, members of the public were invited to make presentations to the OMB. Some of these were not to the point; representatives of the Ward Two Businessmens' Association said that they thought it was a waste of money to divide the city into 11 new wards, and it was going to cost $1,500 for the association to change all its stationery, its membership forms and so on.

Helen Johnston and Ben Grys, two aldermen who had lobbied for small changes in the city clerk's proposal only to see City Council throw out their suggestions when the issue became contentious, appeared before the OMB and urged small changes in the strip plan which, apparently, they assumed it was going to adopt. Mr. Grys, discussing the west end rearrangement that he wanted, let the cat out of the bag when he pointed out that the change he proposed would make the two wards affected "come within 1,500 votes . . . er . . . population of each other."

Another elected representative to make a statement

to the OMB was Maurice Lister, a school trustee for Ward Two. The Board of Education had officially declared itself in favor of the strip plan; Mr. Lister made it clear that he was speaking for himself. What he said was courageous and honest; the only other politician who has spoken in such a frank way during the debate on this issue is Charles Caccia who has now formally resigned from City Council.

Mr. Lister said that he has had some experience trying to represent a strip ward much like those proposed for the centre of the city by the strip plan. He said that he has found it virtually impossible to represent both the north and the south ends of his present ward.

This was in marked contrast to the fourth politician who spoke, Alderman Alice Summerville, who burbled about how she has been representing rich and poor in her ward and how she has enjoyed it.

One of the last statements made at the hearing was from Susan Fish, a researcher for the Bureau of Municipal Research. The bureau is an independent, business-financed research organization with no municipal axes to grind. It pointed to three standards which are generally used to judge electoral boundaries, and produced data which made it clear that the block plan is superior to the strip plan.

The city's lawyer found himself at the end of the afternoon with only one last chance to save the city's plan. His strategy was to try to turn what everyone had agreed was the serious weakness of the city's proposal into a strength. We have heard, he said, that the strip plan cuts across natural communities and straddles high and low income areas. I say this is a good thing. It carries on logically from what has gone on in the past. There are strong pressure groups from urban renewal areas who want a voice, he went on. They already have a voice: this is borne out by a perfunctory reading of the daily press. I challenge the evidence, in fact I have heard none, that these areas are not represented, Mr. Fram continued. Is the solution to divide the city socially? Why not ethnically? I think it is most unfortunate to propose boundaries which would break up the Italian community. I think it is wrong for aldermen to represent only low-income people.

Wrong for aldermen to represent only low-income people? Mr. Kennedy interrupted Mr. Fram's summation to ask what was wrong with it.

It is wrong, Mr. Fram said, because it introduces an unsavory class element into municipal politics.

Perhaps a different OMB chairman might have listened to that. Perhaps Mr. Fram was hoping that Mr. Kennedy would suddenly see dangers in city aldermen speaking up strongly for the interests of people who are facing expropriation proceedings, for residents who are being pushed out of their homes by high-rise redevelopment, for the people whose streets the city never quite manages to sweep properly in the summer or plough in winter.

But Mr. Kennedy didn't. Instead he allowed Mr. Fram to destroy his own argument by asking what the difference would be between a system of at-large elections for aldermen and wards drawn so that residents have nothing in common. Mr. Fram answered that there was no difference and the only reason he could think of for retaining wards was that they could cut down on the expenses of city-wide campaigning.

The OMB's decision was announced a few days after the hearing. The brief written decision reviewed the arguments and said that the OMB was selecting the city clerk's block plan over the strip plan recommended by the politicians.

* * *

The city politicians could hardly believe what had happened to them. They had lost a fight as important as this one. Consternation was their first reaction; fear was their second. Many knew that the block plan would force them to run in largely-unfamiliar wards in an election only five months away. Their chances might prove no better than those of the candidates already lining up to run against them.

City Council acted quickly. The provincial legislation allows for appeals from OMB decisions to the cabinet. A special meeting of City Council was called. The transcript of the day-long hearing was obtained. At their meeting, the politicians complained at length about Kennedy, about newspaper editorial writers, about troublemakers from Don Vale and Trefann and about the disgusting articles I was writing and the *Globe and Mail* was publishing.

According to City Hall gossip, when the council's appeal got to the Ontario cabinet the decision was put into the hands of the two Toronto cabinet ministers, Allan Grossman and Allan Lawrence, along with municipal affairs minister D'Arcy McKeough. Grossman, a former Toronto alderman, strongly supported the strip plan. Lawrence, so the gossip went, favored the block plan. So did McKeough. However it happened, the cabinet rejected the city's appeal. And the aldermen had no alternative left but to look for as safe a constituency as they could find in these extremely unfortunate circumstances.

Chapter Three
Urban Renewal:
City Planning and Local Politics

Urban renewal in Toronto came to a halt at the end of 1966 when city planners and politicians failed to get an expropriation plan approved for the Trefann Court area in central Toronto. The Trefann plan was in fact formally passed by City Council, but there were strong objections from area residents at a time when a civic election was impending and the politicians did not dare take the one last step necessary in order to get it implemented.

After that confrontation, urban renewal in Toronto came to mean not demolishing large numbers of old houses but rather interminable discussions and disputes among politicians and residents. Plans were drawn up in 1967-69 in two other renewal areas, Don Vale and Kensington, and after about two years of refusing to abandon the old plan for Trefann while refusing to draw up a new one, the city politicians and officials withdrew the original Trefann proposal. They did not, however, begin working on a new plan for Trefann. Instead, they let residents stew. The area remained designated for urban renewal; the city's site office remained open and staffed; residents had no incentive to repair or renovate because there was still a good prospect that their homes would be torn down; no one was interested in buying a house in the neighborhood because of the uncertainty. Trefann residents learned that expropriation was not the only way the city could harm people with its urban renewal policies. No doubt they were expected to draw from their experiences the conclusion that perhaps expropriation might not be quite as bad as some other alternatives.

In Toronto's two other urban renewal planning areas, however, City Council agreed to set up special planning committees of representatives of local residents' and businessmen's associations and elected politicians. City officials reported to the Kensington Urban Renewal Committee; they sat as members on the Don Vale Working Committee. These bodies began to work out detailed plans, and by mid-1969 agreed planning policies had been developed for Kensington, and a detailed plan had been prepared for Don Vale by the Working Committee.

It was clear from the beginning that people in Don Vale and Kensington were interested in quite different plans for their neighborhoods than the city's planners had traditionally produced for urban renewal areas. The participation of residents led to plans which conserved, strengthened and improved existing neighborhoods instead of destroying them by expropriation. The planning policies which were developed went far beyond housing conditions to consider public works like roads and lanes, services like garbage collection and police, and community facilities like recreation centres and schools, but these plans also provided encouragement and financial programs to persuade homeowners to repair and renovate their houses. The biggest problem in these areas was to make up for the disruption in normal repair and renovation work caused by the years of uncertainty and the threat of urban renewal and expropriation.

The detailed Don Vale plan was approved by the Working Committee in mid-1969. By that time, however, a federal government freeze on funds for implementing urban renewal plans was almost a year old. Federal politicians had finally in 1968 caught up with the residents of urban renewal areas and realized the sense of their complaints that expropriation-style renewal was both harmful to people and needlessly expensive. The question which was unanswered in 1968 and 1969 when the federal freeze was taking effect was whether the federal government would change its urban renewal legislation and would fund plans which dealt more efficiently and more successfully with the problems of urban renewal areas. Even if the federal government was not willing to get involved in a huge new round of expenditures on new-style renewal projects across the country, it clearly had an obligation to areas like Trefann Court and Don Vale, whose residents had suffered from several years of urban renewal planning when it looked like the only thing in store for them was eventual expropriation.

While plans were being drawn up in Kensington and Don Vale and while nothing was being done in Trefann Court, city officials and politicians were learning that the residents' groups in these areas were very independent-minded and not prepared to let themselves be pushed around. When, for example, the Don Vale plan was sent to City Council by the Don Vale Working Committee, the politicians deferred discussion for several months and city officials submitted lukewarm reports on it even though they had been involved in drawing it up. The reaction of the residents' association in Don Vale was not to smile and sit back and wait for the politicians to do what they thought was right. The association protested and picketed about the delays.

In order to deal with these independent and quite powerful local associations, city officials and politicians encouraged the formation of rival groups in urban renewal areas. This policy was aimed at creating an impression of disunity and dissension, so that politicians and officials would be able to move much more freely and answer the complaints of local groups by saying that groups complained no matter what they did.

In September-October 1969, all these issues came to a

head when the mayor arranged a conference at City Hall between city politicians and the federal and provincial ministers in charge of urban renewal. After the meeting was set up and before it took place, it apparently became obvious to city officials that they would be leaving themselves open to serious criticism from the provincial and federal politicians if they left Trefann Court where it was — designated for urban renewal but with no plan drawn up and none underway. The city lost no time in getting planning going again in Trefann, but in doing so the politicians made only the slightest of bows in the direction of local participation in the planning process. I reported on the meeting of the Board of Control when this matter was discussed.

September 8, 1969

Trefann Planning and the Board of Control

The Board of Control had before it on September 3 a recommendation that Development Commissioner Graham Emslie draw up a new plan for Trefann Court. No terms of reference were proposed for this plan; no instructions of any kind were given regarding what sort of plan it should be or how it should be drawn up.

Mr. Emslie had every reason to think he was being asked to draw up whatever plan he wanted. Certainly he was not being told to do it with local residents, or even to consult with them. In similar situations in Don Vale and Kensington, in contrast, City Council and its committees after elaborate and lengthy negotiations among city politicians, officials and residents laid down detailed formal guidelines and terms of reference for the plan and established committees of politicians, officials and residents to do the planning work. Without these conditions, residents of those areas would have refused to have anything to do with the city's planning. Yet the Housing, Fire and Legislation Committee saw no reason to attach any conditions or terms or instructions of any kind to its motion.

The Trefann Court Residents' Association had appeared as a delegation before the board and said in its brief that if the city was going to decide unilaterally to go ahead with its planning with no consultation with local people, the association wanted to see the whole urban renewal business for its area called off.

The reaction of all four controllers to this brief was to explain their reasons individually for wanting to see planning go ahead in Trefann on the proposed basis. Though none of them said so, in fact they were explaining why they were not prepared to give the same amount of participation and control over planning to people in Trefann that they had agreed to for local groups in Kensington and Don Vale. They were also explaining why they were not prepared to lay down stringent guidelines of the kind which were found necessary in these other areas to ensure that the desired participation would take place and that the plan would not be harmful to local people.

Controller Margaret Campbell's explanation of her position was the most astonishing. Controller Campbell has strongly supported the demands of Don Vale and Kensington residents for control over planning for their areas and has established a reputation in these and other areas of the city as the one politician who understands the meaning and implications of placing more planning power in the hands of local groups and committees of city politicians and representatives of area associations. Trefann is, however, a different matter for Controller Campbell.

"Your committee did not make a snap decision that night, I can tell you that," she told Board of Control as the controller who sits on the Housing, Fire and Legislation Committee, which had made the recommendation that planning in Trefann should start. "It was a firm decision because we were tired of trying to meet with people who simply refused to show any kind of creative effort in the area at all over all these long months."

Several times Controller Campbell came back to this complaint: the Trefann residents' association had refused to get down to work on a new plan. Our officials, she said at one point, "have never been able to get to grips with this one group in trying to rework the plan."

What Controller Campbell considers coming to grips with residents or making a "creative effort" is, of course, impossible to say. The most recent proposal by the Trefann association to get the city to act on planning for its area was that independent planners be hired who would work with local residents and with the city's planners.

This is only the most recent in a long series of proposals which the association has made for a new plan for its area which go back to November, 1966. Virtually all of those have been ignored by the politicians.

The independent planners' proposal was discussed by the association's executives with Mr. Emslie and Planning Commissioner Dennis Barker in the spring of 1969 and they gave informal approval of the idea. Association secretary Edna Dixon wrote an official letter asking City Council approval of this proposal on May 9 and brought it up in subsequent correspondence. Yet Board of Control passed the letters on without comment to the housing committee and that committee has yet to discuss this request. Having independent planners work with local residents appears to be a sensible proposal, but attempts to implement the suggestion have been frustrated by politicians. For Controller Campbell, however, this attitude of the association (and other transgressions she attributed to the group) somehow disqualifies it from any claims to participation in planning.

It was not quite clear that Controller Fred Beavis understood the significance of the proposal that the board was discussing; in his view, the only question seemed to be how soon the whole area could be torn down. Controller Beavis (who said the same thing three years ago about Don Mount) talked about the many houses in Trefann that "should have been demolished for safety's sake," but he did not explain why the minimum health and housing standards and other bylaws being enforced by the city in Trefann were not adequate to deal with immediate threats to safety.

He argued that a new plan should be drawn up for Trefann quickly and said he would fight to see it adopted. "When we get the reports, I think it's up to us to make some kind of representation to the higher levels of government and to make sure that this plan is implemented." And a final point: "If we get through this winter without any serious fires, well, it'll be by the grace of God." Implicit in what he was saying was Controller Beavis' view that there were no fine points to be settled about a Trefann plan and certainly not much room in its preparation for people who have a record of being opposed to demolition of their area.

Controller June Marks began her speech by reminding everyone that she, too, used to live south of Bloor Street. Her complaint about Trefann residents was that the association is not the strong, independent local group it appears to be. Rather, it and the people of the area are being used by someone Controller Marks referred to obliquely as "a young man." Controller Marks was referring to John Sewell, lawyer for the association for the past two and a half years and now an aldermanic candidate in Ward Seven, part of Controller Marks' old Ward Two. She underlined Mr. Sewell's activities to the board by recounting how she had encountered him at a meeting in the Sherbourne and Carlton Streets area where high-rise redevelopment of some old houses is scheduled. "For no apparent reason," she said, "this young man is going from area to area, in advance now, *in advance*" — to stir up trouble. Controller Marks nevertheless went on to reassure Trefann residents she and the city's politicians would listen to their views regarding a plan, but it seemed clear she didn't guarantee to pay much attention to what the residents' association said.

Controller Marks' most surprising statement was that, in spite of her opinion of the association, Trefann residents should not worry about whether the new plan protects their interests. "As far as the citizens are concerned, a plan would naturally have to come before this committee and if we haven't, in five years, heard all that the citizens want for that area, then in Controller Lamport's words on another occasion, shame on us. We will know when we see the plan whether these are plans that the people will want or not want."

Like Controller Campbell, Controller Marks was saying that local participation in urban renewal planning could not be allowed when the politicians do not like the local groups or their views on policy. She went a little further, however, by arguing that everything was all right because the politicians knew best.

Mayor William Dennison missed the discussion of this matter. The fourth member of the board to express his view was Controller Lamport. Alone among the four, he expressed the usual enthusiasm for "participation" but made it clear he had no time for any new-style participation where local residents actually sit down at the same table as city officials and politicians.

"While this is an association," he said, referring to the Trefann group, "it is difficult to be sure if the association does speak for everybody, even though they may all be members of the association. I would welcome an opportunity — and surely this is public participation if there ever was any — that we poll, as the Planning Board does on other items . . . that we have the area polled." Controller Lamport anticipated that a poll of residents would show that they weren't interested in urban renewal, but would prefer city encouragement of private development.

If the question were put in those terms, considering Trefann's experience with urban renewal planning in the past few years, no doubt Controller Lamport is right.

Board of Control did not approve the recommendation that Mr. Emslie proceed to draw up a new plan for Trefann, but that was only because it didn't have a cost estimate in front of it. Instead, it spent its time developing excuses and explanations for the approval which it gave at a special meeting five days later. After three years of doing nothing, suddenly the politicians were in a tremendous rush to get on with a new plan for Trefann Court.

Mr. Emslie will no doubt talk very nicely to the

association and will do his best to let everyone know he tried hard to get them to express their views on what the plan should be. Yet in the absence of any guarantees, any terms of reference, any formal commitment that anyone will pay any attention to what it says and in view of the reception its positive planning proposals have received, it is hard to see the residents' association agreeing to have anything to do with drawing up the plan.

So the city is ensuring that it will have another fight on its hands when this plan is prepared. And the controllers have demonstrated that their fine words (and their not totally unrelated deeds in Kensington and Don Vale) about citizen participation apply only when and where the politicians choose to apply them.

* * *

Trefann Court has had its share of disputes between local residents about what should happen in their area. These disputes, sometimes a genuine reflection of different interests and sometimes a result of the activities of city politicians and officials anxious to create an impression of local dissension, are extremely helpful to the city administration. They justify the argument that local people cannot solve their own problems, and that City Hall must therefore do it for them.

As soon as it was clear in 1967-68 that residents' organizations in urban renewal areas were posing a serious challenge to the powers of the city administration, rival groups appeared to contest the legitimacy of the major associations in the Trefann and Don Vale areas. There was never any serious attempt made by the newspapers or by anyone at City Hall to investigate what lay behind this local factionalism or to see whether the most vocal people in these groups were in fact speaking for anyone besides themselves in the areas they claimed to represent. Apparently the purposes of the politicians and officials were served by the simple fact that there was more than one citizens' group in these areas, and that the groups disagreed with each other about what city policy should be regarding urban renewal.

It was as background to the meeting organized by the mayor and attended by provincial and federal cabinet ministers responsible for urban renewal in October 1969 that I wrote an article which discussed the internal politics of these citizen organizations. I was writing while I was an active member of one Don Vale association, the Don Vale Association of Homeowners and Residents, and this fact was always given great weight by the people at City Hall who didn't like what I was saying. But no one has ever suggested that there was any serious inaccuracy in these descriptions of the different groups in urban renewal areas.

October 13, 1969

The local politics of urban renewal

Each urban renewal area in Toronto has its major residents' group. In Trefann, this is the Trefann Court Residents' Association. In Don Vale, it is the Don Vale Association of Homeowners and Residents. In Kensington, it is the Kensington Area Residents' Association. These major groups have several common features. Membership in them is open; anyone who is a homeowner or a tenant in the area can join. They have a president and quite a large executive group which keeps in touch with what is happening at City Hall and meets together regularly, once every week or two. The groups' officers and executive are elected annually at an open public meeting which any local resident can attend and where nominations are open and everyone votes. The executive groups make their decisions by majority votes; the presidents have no special authority. In addition, Kensington and Trefann have full-time community workers associated with them who work under the direction of the executive groups. Major problems are discussed and policy decisions are made not by the executive group but by public area meetings. When detailed planning questions came up in Don Vale and

Kensington, the major residents' group organized special street and block meetings and the people attending these meetings decided what their association's policy on these questions would be.

All three groups have been around for about three years. During this time, their major policy on urban renewal has often been a word-for-word repetition of the virtually unanimous view of people in their areas. This was certainly the case, for instance, in late 1966 when Trefann Court was fighting the city planners' proposal for demolishing their area. It was true in mid-1967 when Trefann and Don Vale were supporting the last-ditch stand by four Don Mount homeowners for home-for-a-home expropriation compensation. Virtually everyone in Don Vale was unanimous that the plans proposed by the city in 1966-67 for their area were completely unacceptable.

Sometimes, though, the executives of these major groups have gone off on side-tracks advocating policies where they do not have unanimous or even sometimes majority support in their area. In Don Vale, for example, enforcement of extra-high housing standards by the city, along with 90-100 per cent of the cost to be paid by grants to pay virtually the entire cost of the necessary work, was proposed by the association executive as a viable policy in 1967-68. In fact, there is little doubt that area residents regarded this price tag as one which demonstrated the impossibility of the policy, and that they found the policy unacceptable on any terms. The way these groups are run, however, ensures that there is constant feedback from ordinary residents to executive members at public meetings, through normal neighborhood contacts, at street and block meetings, and through the choice of officers. Within each group, the tendency of some people to go off in whatever policy direction they personally think right is constantly being counteracted by the tendency of others to say and do only what people at street meetings and area meetings instruct them to say.

All this, city officials and politicians should know, and most of them do know. But they know too that they themselves are always claiming to speak for the people when the people, in fact, amount to their relatives, newspaper reporters, other city politicians and business associates. So they are cynical about claims of local groups to do any better at consulting with their constituencies. They are also aware that the more seriously they take the claims of these groups, the less important and less powerful their function in city government becomes. The result is that people at City Hall pretend to see little or no difference between these major local groups and the opposition groups which also exist in urban renewal areas.

In Don Vale, the opposition groups are the Don Vale Property Owners and the Don Vale Tenants' Association. In Trefann, they are the Trefann Neighbors' and Tenants' Association and the Businessmen's Association. These opposition groups also have some common characteristics. They too have executives, though these tend to consist of one to four people rather than the ten to twenty of the major groups. The executives are self-appointed. They make "association policy" as they wish. If the opposition groups have any members at all, these turn out to be residents who have at some time signed a petition or a statement apparently supporting the basic position of the executive group. Rarely, if ever, are public or members' meetings held and, when they are, members are asked not to instruct the executive on policy matters but to endorse whatever its views are at the time. Individual members who disagree are generally thrown out. These opposition groups are, in other words, run from the top down. Often they are nothing but a top. The Don Vale Tenants' Association, for instance, has one tenant member who works along with one or two volunteer workers. The other opposition groups are similar in size.

These groups are often set up and always continue to exist only because the city hall political world is so friendly to them. In some cases, in fact, the politicians have had friends and associates who live outside the area concerned set up organizations which then claim to represent the real views of the people. This is the case regarding the Trefann Neighbors' and Tenants' Association. "Neighbors" turns out to mean ladies from Rosedale. The politicians and officials are very relieved to have these opposition groups around, because the fact that they exist and that they are taken seriously at City Hall helps to weaken the claims of the major urban renewal residents' groups to speak for the vast majority of people in their areas. The opposition groups find that they are being treated very well, and important city hall people are ready to spend long hours listening closely to their views. If City Hall regards them as the legitimate voice of the people, what reason is there to go through the long and difficult procedures of organizing meetings and talking to local people in order to find out what they think?

* * *

In early 1970, the Bureau of Municipal Research in Toronto published the findings of a research project it had conducted into citizen participation and citizens' groups in Toronto city politicians were interviewed by the Board's researchers, and according to their report 100 per cent of the politicians interviewed "agreed that the [neighborhood] groups are not representative of the neighborhoods they purport to represent and 60 per cent felt that the groups often act contrary to the public interest." Given this climate of opinion about neighborhood organizations in general, it is easy to see why opposition groups in urban renewal areas — with their incontestable merit of almost always being on the right side in the politicians' eyes — are as well treated as they are. It is also easy to see why the attempts of major groups in renewal areas to act responsibly and in a representative way are so unsuccessful at affecting the politicians.

Chapter Four
Downtown Kids and Downtown Schools

Kids and schools are a subject of widespread and intense interest to many people who are generally not affected by politics and political matters. Perhaps this stems from the crucial place in people's lives which the school system occupies. It is through the school system that the realities of the social and political world reach right into people's private lives, into the lives of their children who ought (if what everyone says about equality and freedom means anything) to be starting out from the same place no matter what the social class, the status, the income or the neighborhood of their parents.

The people I know in downtown Toronto, in areas like Don Vale and Trefann Court, seem to be of two minds about the school system. On one hand, they regard schools, teachers and principals with a respect and deference which they rarely show for people with similar roles in other institutions (judges, mayors, policemen, for instance). It is almost as if their attitude is a throwback, based not on their present experience and situation but a return to when they last had serious contact with these people, when they were themselves pupils in school. On the other hand, people see the school system as an extremely expensive government operation which does not succeed in doing even the most elementary things (like teaching kids to read, or giving kids enough education so they can get a decent job when they get out of school) and is particularly unsatisfactory in what it does for children from low-income working-class neighborhoods.

A good part of the explanation for why parents know so little about what really happens in the schools is that the schools themselves do their best to keep parents ignorant. The virtue of ignorance in their eyes is that it is the easiest and perhaps the most efficient way of keeping parents quiet. What they don't know they won't complain about, must be one of the unspoken mottos of the school system.

Some of the ways this is accomplished are listed in the two articles in this chapter: meaningless or inaccurate descriptions of school programs (the "opportunity classes" discussed in the first article), meaningless reports on student work and progress (like the report cards and diplomas quoted in the second article), encouragement of pseudo-participation by parents in school affairs while firmly discouraging any attempt at real involvement, and the cultivation of false impressions regarding the rights of parents and children.

In 1968 a group of mothers of school-age children in Trefann Court began meeting together to talk about their experiences with the school system and to learn more about what was going on in the schools. By mid-1969 this group was very well-informed about what the Toronto Board of Education says it is doing and what in fact it is doing in the various public and high schools their children were attending. The two articles which I wrote about this group reported on some of the experiences of their children in school, and indicated the analysis of how the school system really works which their meetings and discussions had led them to.

The first article was based on a conversation I had with one of the ladies in the group about her experiences with "opportunity classes" in Park School, a public school which serves Trefann Court and Regent Park.

July 28, 1969

Sandra MacGregor and
Park School's "Opportunity Class"

In Toronto's school system there are more than a hundred special classes which the Board of Education calls "opportunity classes." They are, according to the board's last annual report, for the "educable mentally retarded, 7-13 years of age."

A year ago, the youngest opportunity class at Park School on Shuter Street lost one of its nine pupils to Everdale Place, a private school outside of Toronto run by a group of people who are highly critical of the public school system. At a cost of $1350, one girl has been taken out of a situation where she was classed as "educable mentally retarded" and has gone to a school where the teachers don't take categories and classifications of this kind too seriously.

I asked her mother if she would make a public end-of-the-year report on what has happened to her daughter in her first year at Everdale, and if she would compare this experience with what has been happening to another one of her children who has now spent six years in opportunity classes at Park School. She agreed, but she suggested that her name and that of her daughter be changed because she said that she has no ambition to have a public reputation as a critic of the Board of Education. But they all know me, she said, they will know exactly who it is.

Mrs. MacGregor's first child to be put in an "opportunity class" was Beverley. "Beverley was in Grade Three and she was going into Grade Four and then they decided that she needed special help with her reading. And I said all right, because when I went to school if you needed special help with reading you went to a reading class and this is what I understood it to be. But it wasn't this at all;

it was the opportunity class. And they just left her there.

"When she started out first she was in Miss Tuft's class, that is the younger kids, maybe eight, nine and ten-year-olds. And then when she got to be ten years old she was too old for that class so she went to Miss Ross, I believe it was, for 11 and 12, and then when you got too old for that class you went to Miss Ayleshire's class for 13 and 14.

"She comes home with pencils and papers and crayons, the same as a child from kindergarten or Grade One would do. This is why I get so mad with Beverley. She's been going to school for eight years, and she comes home with crayon pictures."

I asked if she can read.

"Very little, very little, and if she can count up money, she can't add it up properly. Or you give her a column of figures; she can't add that. Like my husband asked her the other day, we were looking at the record, and he asked her to spell Greensleeves. Now she couldn't spell it, and yet Maggie from Grade Two could spell it.

"I asked Beverley's teacher one time, you know, how come she's not progressing. I saved her report cards from the one year to the next year; they were both almost identical in the marks and even the comments were almost identical. And I said to the teachers, now how come, she's been here the two years, this report card says exactly the same thing, she's not brought herself up any. Well, from there they took her out of that class and that's the year when they put her in with Miss Ross, and that's when Miss Ross said that she did such wonderful things. But I couldn't see any difference."

Beverley developed a dislike for school. "She ran away two or three times and she refused to go to school quite a few times. I don't know, she just took a dislike against teachers . . ."

Sandy's story started much the same way. She went to school and was in a normal class in Grade One and Grade Two.

"She went to Grade Two," Mrs. MacGregor said,

"and that's as far as she got. Then they put her in opportunity class. They told me it was on account of her reading, but every time we go over and talk to them they say, 'well, no, no, no, that's not true' and yet they never give me an answer although one time they said that she's this and she's that and she's a little bit mentally disturbed — I mean, you really don't know which way to turn.

"They called me over and I said, 'Well, I would prefer her to stay for two years in the second grade' and they said, well, her teacher said to me, 'Now she'll look very stupid in with the children coming from Grade One', and I said I could care less how stupid she looks, it's the idea that she's the same age as the kids and I would like her to stay in Grade Two. They said, well, she needed help in her reading, and going through my mind was all the problems I had with Beverley going into this opportunity class and I thought, 'Well, I don't want the same thing for her.'

"And then they said they would leave her the one year and then she would go on to the regular grade. They didn't do that; they just put her in there and that was the end of it."

I asked whether the "opportunity class" had improved Sandy's reading.

"It seemed that rather than bringing her up in just her reading or anything, it didn't work that way, not as far as I was concerned; they say, well, yes, she's progressing, she's progressing but as far as her report cards and her marks she never got a thing better than what she got when she was in Grade Two.

"She never learned a blessed thing. All she did was the same thing, to color paper, you know, with crayon pictures, that was about all she ever learned.

"She never brought a book home. I went over to the school and I asked the teachers, 'Does she have any type of reader? ' 'No.' 'Does she have any kind of a workbook that I could help her with? ' 'Oh, no, her printing is fine,' and I said, 'What about her reading? ' and she said, 'Well, when she prints, she has to learn to read from printing' and I said 'How could she learn to print if she doesn't know how to read? ' And the teachers just looked at me and she said, 'Well, we let them go at their own normal speed.' And that was it; she never learned anything."

It was at this point, after Beverley had been in the Park School opportunity class for five years and Sandy for two that a community worker in the Trefann Court area where Mrs. MacGregor lives suggested that perhaps the MacGregors should consider sending Beverley and Sandy to Everdale to see whether a school of that kind could be of any use to them. At first it looked as if enough money could be found to pay for both girls, but in the end it proved difficult enough to find enough for one and the family decided that Sandy was the one who should go.

It was not an easy decision, since it meant that Sandy would be living away from home for ten months of the year, and Mrs. MacGregor had serious doubts.

"At first I felt so bad because she used to cry every week, and I said to her, each week when she used to come home for the weekend, I'd say, 'Try it for one more week,' but after she was there for a month I couldn't keep her home if I wanted to. She felt very strange at first but then she got in with the children from the school and she found out that they were going back and forth on weekends and she got two or three pals of her own and I mean instead of leaving here at seven o'clock she used to leave at six o'clock so she could wait the extra hour in the bus terminal with the kids."

Mrs. MacGregor says there is no comparison between the teachers at Park and those at Everdale. "The ones at Everdale, they seem more like family than teachers . . . I know I was very disturbed up to the time that Sandy's teacher came to talk to me about her, I really felt bad because I didn't feel as though she was progressing — I really didn't know what to think. And after she left I felt much better."

Sandy has been bringing home Grade Five math books, and after she had done her math homework Mrs. MacGregor asked her older son to check them to see if the answers were right. He said they were.

"I mean this really made me mad, when she came in with Grade Five books and then over at the school they said, well, she wasn't good enough for Grade Three."

What about reading? "At the end of the year, when I phoned, Sandy's teacher said that Sandy had really advanced far beyond what she had expected of her. She didn't figure that in one year she would really come up as far as she had, and she was quite pleased at her progress and everything else at school."

Sandy now brings home books from school which she reads, real books, not story books for six-year-olds.

Mrs. MacGregor is obviously pleased with what is happening, pleased with the work Sandy is doing and with the school, the teachers, and the opportunities it is providing Sandy. Sandy has changed, according to her mother: "Her whole outlook on life seems to be different."

Meanwhile, Beverley will be spending her last year in the opportunity class at Park next year; at the age of 14 she graduates automatically to a special vocational school, Eastdale, which takes many, perhaps all, the girls who have previously been in opportunity classes.

"The Everdale people sent us a brochure," Mrs. MacGregor said, "stating that they are in financial difficulty; they say that in a couple of years they'd like to do away with the fee so just anybody could come, rather than just from wealthy families." Meanwhile, the school itself requires $35,000 in addition to students' fees to finance its operations over the next year.

Raising next year's fee for Sandy is a pressing problem to the MacGregors, and it puts into focus a number of larger questions. Why should parents have to pay $1350 a year to have their child go to a school where the teachers apparently are successful at teaching her to read and do math? Is it the fault of Beverley MacGregor that she has spent eight years in school, six years receiving the special attention which is supposed to be part of an "opportunity class," and she still cannot read properly? Is the "opportunity class" program really just a garbage dump measure for children who are defined as "retarded" at the age of seven and then forgotten until they are sent off to another school at 13? Do the people at Park School claim they made a mistake with Sandy? If they did, have they made a mistake about Beverley? And what about the other children in the school's three "opportunity classes"?

According to Mrs. MacGregor, one of the administrators at Park School has told her that she is a shit-disturber. There is no doubt that she has not let the school alone to do whatever they think best with her children. What has happened to Sandy suggests that she had very good reason to ask questions, even if it does make some teachers and principals feel uncomfortable.

* * *

The second article reported on what the mothers in the Trefann group said at a press conference they held in August when they announced that one of their number, Noreen Gaudette, was planning to run for a seat on the Board of Education in the December city elections. At the press conference the group members talked about what had happened to their kids in school and what they had learned from their year of meeting together and talking to Board of Education officials and teachers. They left no room for doubt about how badly the schools have been serving their families.

August 25, 1969

"Her daughter got good manners in woodwork"

"There was a time," said Mrs. Phyllis Tomlinson at last week's press conference, "when we sent the kids to school and we thought, well, they're the Board of Education, they know what they're doing. But now we aren't so sure."

At the press conference a long series of specific worries and complaints came up: report cards, opportunity classes, reading levels, ungraded classes, admission to senior schools. On their own these were cause for concern. But from their experiences with the public school system the Trefann mothers have come to the disturbing conclusion that their children are not getting the same quality of education as are children in wealthier, middle-class areas, and that many teachers and officials of the Board of Education consider that they and their children are inferior.

Many of the things the members of the group are concerned about stem from the experience of their own children in the schools they attend: Park, Regent Park, Castle Frank, Eastdale, Central Tech. They have noticed, for instance, that it appears to take a very long time for teachers at Park School to get to the point of teaching children to read. Some pupils spend their first three years in school doing little if any reading, but doing a lot of drawing. Said Mrs. Gaudette: "It takes you three years to learn how to draw. You go to junior kindergarten, senior kindergarten, Grade One and then in Grade Two you start to read."

They have also noticed that their children are often behind children at other schools in how quickly they are being taught to read. "I've got a grandson in Grade One at Deer Park," said Mrs. Gaudette, "and he's already through the first two readers. And here's my own kid, his uncle, in Grade Two at Park going on to Three, and he's still on the first book that my grandson is past."

Several of the mothers have had experience with the opportunity classes in Park School where children are sent, usually, they've been told, because they have reading problems which can be corrected only in the special "opportunity classes." But it never seems to work that way. "I've got two kids," said Mrs. Sarah Hayward. "The oldest one is in opportunity. The smallest one in Grade Two can outread her and outspell her and she's 12 years old. The little one's only eight, and she can do more than the 12-year-old who's been in opportunity for two years to smarten up with her reading. You're supposed to go into opportunity to learn how to read, but it doesn't seem to make any difference."

Last year, Park School had a meeting for parents to inform them that classes in the first four years of school to the end of Grade Three were to become ungraded. The members of the mothers' group are concerned about how this will cut them off from information about how well their children are really progressing. "We're worried about it," said Mrs. Tomlinson, "because for three or four years our children are going to be there and we won't know what they're doing, what level they're at, and you can't find out from the school because they're so evasive. They know everything, they've got everything under control and we're just a bunch of . . . idiots."

Members of the group can't understand the basis on which the school decides whether to promote children, to fail them, or to put them in opportunity classes. Frequently teachers tell parents that a child has been moved to an opportunity class because he was taller than classmates and so would feel "stupid" unless moved. The result is that parents worry when their children are bigger than average for their age. Said Mrs. Tomlinson of her eldest son: "When he turned 12 and he was so big I panicked and I thought this is the end of him. They'll send him to some vocational course. They'll figure that he'll just feel stupid."

Another group member, Mrs. Barbara Dawson, reported on how a Park teacher had explained why he had promoted Mrs. Gaudette's son to Grade Eight even though the boy was having serious problems with his work. "He's a good athlete," Mrs. Dawson quoted the teacher as saying of Mrs. Gaudette's son, "and he knows how to play baseball. He'll catch on to his arithmetic."

Several of the mothers referred to the apparently glowing report card comments they received from teachers. Mrs. Tomlinson showed us the report card for her son in Grade Eight last year. "Arthur has had an exceptionally good year academically," it said in the space for teachers' comments. "He has been most helpful and cooperative in extra-curricular school functions. He has been an asset to the class and the graduating class of '69." "Anybody would be real proud of it," Mrs. Tomlinson said, "if they didn't know that it doesn't mean anything. This is my son's report card, and yet the guidance teacher tells me that he shouldn't go to Jarvis Collegiate because he didn't have it in him. But this is his report card. There's not one bad mark on it, though he didn't stand first in his class, mind you. But all those fancy words don't mean a thing."

The women in the group have learned that Park School guidance teachers do not have final authority in deciding what high school a student should go to, although one of them suggested at a meeting of parents that he did. He advises most students to choose vocational and technical courses; of the 27 regular students in Arthur Tomlinson's Grade Eight class, 26 passed their year. Only five are going on to academic courses. The others are taking technical and vocational courses. "We went to the Board of Education and the guidance teacher was there and we brought this right out and they said no, it was up to the children's marks," said Mrs. Tomlinson. "If they passed Grade Eight they could go any place they liked. But this isn't what they lead you to believe when you go to the school. You get the idea you have no say and the Board of Education is going to decide."

Members of the group are concerned about Eastdale, a high school for girls where many of the girls who reach 14 in Park School's opportunity classes seem to go. Said Mrs. Eleanor Guerin, whose daughter graduated from Eastdale this June: "You should see the Eastdale report card." "Her daughter got good manners in woodwork," said Mrs. Gaudette. "Honest to goodness. It says 'Woodwork' and then it says 'good manners.'"

At Eastdale, said Mrs. Hayward, "you get diplomas which qualify you for putting cherries in bottles and stringing tennis racquets."

Mrs. Guerin's daughter graduated from Eastdale in June with a diploma which stated that she had taken four years of academic and vocational courses. Unfortunately neither Mrs. Guerin's daughter nor many of the other girls in Trefann who have attended Eastdale have found that their high school background has given them any useful skills. Like her, they have been unable to find jobs when they get out of school at 16 or 17.

It may appear that these worries and criticisms of the school system arise not so much from what is actually happening in the schools as from a lack of information and understanding among parents about what the schools are really doing. Certainly the most striking fact about this group of Trefann mothers is that they have taken an intense interest in what was going on in the schools for the last year. They have had countless meetings with Park School teachers; they have visited other schools; they have met Board of Education officials; and Mrs. Gaudette has even visited a special training course for teachers going to teach in "slum" schools.

They have become very well informed about the school system, and have tried to learn as much as they could. They started out, as Mrs. Tomlinson explained, confident that the Board of Education knew what it was doing. However, as they learned more about the schools and as they encountered teachers and officials, doubts began to crystallize. What was certainly most disturbing was that they began to feel that many of the teachers, the experts, and the officials assumed that their children were going to do badly in school, that they were not as bright or as capable as other children.

They were being put in the category of "slum kids" and the "culturally deprived," and this was regarded as sufficient to explain why so many of them couldn't read, had to go to opportunity classes, found themselves failing in the early grades and ended up in dead-end technical courses at schools where they would receive no academic standing after four years' work.

"As soon as you put your kids into school," said Mrs. Tomlinson, "they start hitting them with this negative approach, that they're never going to amount to anything. They don't say it right out, but it's there."

"Of course this doesn't go on in all the schools," said

Mrs. Gaudette. "People wouldn't stand for it."

Teachers and school officials may not make their view explicit, but they certainly have been pretty frank about it in some of their encounters with the members of the group. Mrs. Tomlinson at one point complained to a guidance teacher at Park School that he was trying to talk her son into going to a technical high school when he was perfectly capable of going to an academic school. "He told me that I have a negative attitude," she said, "and I told him that he had a negative attitude. He kept saying to me, 'But what if he drops out? ' I kept saying 'Don't talk about him dropping out.' "

At one meeting a Park School guidance teacher and social worker once compared Park to a "good school" and then cited Deer Park as an example of what he meant by good. "That's when I started to get hostile to the school," Mrs. Tomlinson said. "I thought that if Deer Park School is better than Park School, then I want my kids taken out and sent to Deer Park School where they would be going to a better school."

"Since we're in what they call a slum," Mrs. Dawson said, "they put all our kids down to the bottom no matter how smart or how bright they are."

"We'd be darn fools to move to a better district and try to live in one room just so our kids could go to a good school. We shouldn't have to," said Mrs. Tomlinson. "We shouldn't have to. We should have it right here."

And that is why Noreen Gaudette is running for election as a school trustee. "We are not interested in making a career out of politics," says the group's press statement, "but we do want to improve the education of our children." What qualifies her and the other members of the small group of Trefann mothers to try to do this is that they have learned, slowly and painfully, something about how the school system which serves their area works. They know from their experience some of the specific places where improvements are needed. As far as they can see, as their press statement points out, no one else seems to be doing anything about it. So Mrs. Gaudette and the other women are trying to do something themselves.

* * *

Chapter Five
Private Landlords and Public Housing

Many of the people who rent relatively low-cost houses in the central part of cities like Toronto have long had a stable and secure relationship with their landlords. The houses have been owned not for speculation but for income, by landlords who were likely to keep them for decades. Once a tenant established himself as reliable, he could count not only on being able to live in his house for years, but on paying rent lower that what he would have to pay if he were to rent a similar house from a landlord who did not know him. Nor was that the only security the tenant had. If a landlord decided to sell a tenant's house (something which happened mostly when the owner had died and his estate was being settled) the tenant was usually given (and often took up) first option to purchase the house at a reasonable asking price.

In some parts of central Toronto this situation continues. The Wellesley Cottages in Don Vale off Wellesley Street, for instance, built in the 1850's by an owner who intended to rent them for income, are still in the hands of one absentee owner. One of the tenants, a lady of about 75, was born in the Wellesley Cottages and has lived there, first with her family, then with her husband, as a tenant all her life. The situation of the tenants in the Cornwall-Oak area was similar, prior to their expropriation by the Board of Education in 1968.

Generally, however, instability in the real estate market in the central part of the city, created by speculation, by the enormous capital gains available through land redevelopment, and by public projects and programs like urban renewal and highway building, have put an end to this arrangement between landlord and long-term tenant. The cumulative effect of these changes on the supply side of the private housing market and the steadily increasing demand for housing accompanying the city's population growth is that privately-owned low-cost rental housing is becoming more and more difficult to find. As this happens, the importance of the one alternative available for low-income families — public housing, where rents are subsidized and vary according to income instead of the quality of the housing occupied — becomes greater. In mid-1969, in fact, the only hope of a family with three or four kids earning $400 a month to have decent housing at a rent they could afford in Toronto — if they did not happen to be renting a house on the private market already — was to be admitted to public housing.

The articles in this chapter describe the experiences of about 20 families who were evicted in mid-1969 from the houses they were renting. The landlords were about to redevelop their houses using the newest redevelopment technique to appear in the Toronto real estate market: turning "slum houses" for low-income families into "town houses" for middle-income, middle-class families. The evicted families found that the only alternative available to them was to try to get themselves admitted to public housing. This time, however, these prospective customers of the Ontario Housing Corporation, the city's major public housing agency, did not act in the usual way, going one by one to plead for decent housing from OHC officials. Instead, they organized themselves as a group, with the help of John Sewell, one of Trefann Court's community workers, and they dealt with OHC by negotiating and bargaining rather than pleading for themselves as individual cases. The way that OHC dealt with this situation and these tenants proved to be an excellent example of how government agencies and public institutions react to attempts by people who have been unorganized and politically powerless to organize themselves.

June 9, 1969

Berkeley Street:
Thirteen evictions for thirteen boutiques

So-called town houses, renovated and new, have been around Toronto for some time. The renovated ones are small, centrally located, and usually semi-detached if they're not in a row. Before they were converted, working-class people lived in them and outsiders who didn't know anything about them thought of them as "slums."

The transformation of the houses of an area begins with the advance guard of the middle class: architects, artists, and interior designers. They proclaim by their presence that an area has become fashionable. Soon to follow are professors, lawyers, doctors, advertising men, teachers, even businessmen.

Town houses have had a good press and are well-regarded by most people concerned with urban problems. They involve a minimum of $5,000 to $10,000 being spent on physical rehabilitation of houses that often appeared old and rundown and, since the result looks neat and sparkling clean (as it does on Belmont Street, Wellesley Avenue, and Clarence Square) who can seriously doubt that it's a good thing?

Berkeley Street, between King and Adelaide, a short block of 13 houses on the east side of the street with a firehall and a commercial building on the west side, is about to be renovated. The houses have been bought by a partnership of half a dozen people who plan to refurbish their exteriors and to turn them into shops. Six or seven will be kept by the group of purchasers; the others will be sold.

The Berkeley Street operation is typical of how town houses are created; the only unusual thing about it is that the renovated houses will not be lived in but will be used, at least at the start, for shops.

Involved in the Berkeley Street operation is Joan Burt, an architect employed by the new owners, who has been involved in several other projects where houses have been rehabilitated. Miss Burt said the Berkeley houses would be turned into boutiques. "They're rather blank-faced and we thought we might try to get the windows to sort of project out a little bit. We're not going to do anything that means that when the people move in they get someone else's personality stamped too heavily all over the front of the houses. We'll do the roof, molding, stucco and front and put in the windows."

I asked about the present condition of the houses. "Poverty," said Miss Burt, "is a mental state. The houses — they're bad, the walls are cracked. Fine, the walls are cracked; it's called newspapers glued on and you paint it white over top — they'd be just stunned at what the right spirit will do for the houses. And I just don't understand why nobody spreads that word around. It's called eight gallons of white paint and please remove the 49 layers of linoleum and everything's grand."

Asked what is to happen to the families now renting the Berkeley houses for $85 a month, Miss Burt said that the new owners of the street were all very concerned. "The tenants were given notice and I think it went from 45 to 60 days because it depends on when they paid. Four of them have found places to move to; I think a couple more have places to move to but their time isn't up or whatever; the others will move when they find a place. Nobody's pushing them; they'd like to have possession but you can't be unreasonable — they have five, six, seven, eight child-ren."

For every additional unit of downtown, relatively

expensive but high-quality housing provided by town houses, there is one, sometimes two, fewer units of low-cost privately-owned housing which low-income families can afford. To point this out is not to say that town houses are necessarily undesirable; it is to say that they are not the panacea that they are generally regarded to be. In a tight housing market with a serious shortage of low-cost housing (the situation in Toronto in mid-1969) an owner intending to turn a property into a town house creates a serious problem for the people who have been living there, a problem no less serious than if they had been expropriated.

Among the Berkeley Street tenants are Doreen Govereau, Theresa Young, Marie Smith and Donna MacIntyre. A few weeks ago they received notice from Miss Burt's clients that their tenancies would be terminated on June 30. Mrs. Smith has four children and is on welfare. Mrs. MacIntyre, who has four children, earns about $100 a week, but her husband is unemployed. They and the other nine families on the street pay $85 a month for three-bedroom houses. Most of them have been living on Berkeley for several years.

As far as they are concerned, the Berkeley houses as they stand are not a bad bargain. Many are not in the terrible condition Miss Burt describes, though they certainly could be in better shape. The day after I spoke to Miss Burt, I was sitting in Mrs. Smith's kitchen talking with her and Mrs. MacIntyre. The floors there had recently been tiled; the walls were freshly painted; and there were no cracks to be seen. "Everything that's been done in here," Mrs. Smith said, "I did myself. This house was just awful when I moved into it three years ago. It was awful."

The problems of the houses come not from lack of paint. Mrs. Smith mentioned one example: "I had bunks in the bedroom above, and I had finished making the top bunk and I just stuck my head in to make the bottom one when the plaster came down, about so much, and if it had hit me it would have knocked me unconscious. It was so heavy I couldn't lift it off the bed. Now if it had happened at night and the kids were in there, they wouldn't have had a chance."

The Berkeley Street tenants are now facing the problem of having to find somewhere else to live. They have had no luck finding another privately-owned house at a rent they could pay. "I phoned a few," said Mrs. MacIntyre, "and the rents were way above what I can pay." "There is a five-room house in the Danforth area, five rooms for $170,' said Mrs. Smith. "Others are $200, $175, $225. You know, I don't even bother to go and look because at those prices it's a waste of my time. If it was $100, it would be all right."

It's not surprising that rents on the private market are so high. Not only have rents been rising generally, but the supply of relatively inexpensive houses in central Toronto is rapidly being destroyed. Houses are being torn down for schools, office buildings, high-rise apartments. Many of those that aren't being torn down are being converted into housing for the middle class. The cost of 13 new boutiques on Berkeley Street might well prove to be the provincial and federal subsidies required every year for as many additional units of public housing.

Given the cost of privately-owned housing, there is really no practical alternative for people like the Berkeley Street tenants except public housing. In housing provided by the Ontario Housing Corporation, the Berkeley Street families would probably pay from $80 to $120 a month rent depending on their current income level. Though most would be paying somewhat more than on Berkeley, they would be buying higher-quality housing and often a larger home than they have now. Without public housing these families will find themselves crowding into two or three rooms or paying $175 or $200, perhaps 50 or 60 per cent of their income, in rent.

There are, however, many other families in Toronto in much the same situation; there is a serious shortage of public housing; and getting in is a difficult, chancy business.

Mrs. MacIntyre, Mrs. Smith and several other tenants

have been phoning and visiting OHC, trying hard to get some kind of promise of public housing for the end of June. Only Mrs. MacIntyre and another family on the street have been offered OHC housing. "Ontario Housing, plain as I can see," Mrs. Smith told me, "is just stalling because it has apartments ready at Dupont and Avenue Road. I'm not saying how many bedrooms there are because I don't know this, but I know they are ready and I don't know why we're not there. I asked her [someone at OHC] and she said it takes time to process them, and I said 'Well, how much time do you need?' because I was phoning a long time before I had an eviction notice."

The idea that these families might be able to find a nice house at a decent price is so far-fetched and impossible that when Mrs. Smith told me about one she had stumbled on several weeks earlier, it sounded as if she was talking about a dream she had had, not something that could ever have happened in real life: "I went to see this place; they wanted $45 a month. I went up to look at it and it was the most beautiful place you'd ever want to see. It was just that they had the house, they wanted enough to pay the taxes, but they didn't need the money, so they were ·asking $45. But I was too late. Somebody had already taken it."

* * *

Perhaps 200 yards from the houses on Berkeley Street where Joan Burt's clients were going to put their boutiques, ten families in ten houses making up the east side of a small street called Wilkins Avenue were going through an almost identical experience at the same time. They too were being evicted to make way for town housing. The reaction of the Wilkins tenants was to organize themselves as a group, to contact people whom they thought could help (like the minister of the nearby church and John Sewell), and to meet as a group to decide what to do. Their decision was to go in a body to negotiate with OHC about getting admitted to public housing. I wrote an article about what happened when they showed up at OHC's head office, using a tape I had made at that meeting.

June 2, 1969

**Applying for public housing:
bargaining instead of begging**

If you go to apply for public housing to the Ontario Housing Corporation's Toronto office, a building on University Avenue which announces itself as the Zurich Insurance Company, you are sent from the carpet and plush chairs of the reception area on the main floor to a waiting room on the fifth floor. It has shiny vinyl tile floors, one wall almost covered with an enormous face of an old lady (presumably a happy OHC tenant), and benches around the walls for perhaps 15 people. Most of the benches have blue plastic-like cushions; they have no backs. You sit on the benches until someone at one of the two counters is ready to deal with you.

Last Wednesday morning a dozen people living on the east side of Wilkins Avenue (a short street running north off King just east of Parliament) went to OHC's office with a minister, a community worker, a lawyer and a newspaper writer to apply for public housing.

They made the mistake of sitting down in the fifth floor waiting room to await the pleasure of OHC officials. It was a mistake because theirs was no ordinary application for public housing. They were not displaying their miseries, recounting in detail their problems and their impoverished circumstances, requesting, pleading, begging OHC officials to grant them government largesse in the form of publicly subsidized housing. Rather they were experimenting with a new way of applying for public housing: public negotiation between a government agency and a unified group of prospective agency customers.

The normal way to apply for public housing in Toronto is to fill out an application form and to send it to the city's housing registry. The registry sends it to OHC; then OHC sends out a field worker who inspects your housekeeping and reviews your application to ensure that it contains all relevant invformation. OHC then gives you a point rating: so many points for having lots of children, so many for having a low income, so many for being threatened with imminent eviction. You are not told your point rating. OHC housing is supposed to be offered to families who have the most points and so are at the top of the list. You have no way of knowing where you stand on that list, no way of being sure that people who are getting housing in fact have more points than you, no way of ascertaining that your point rating is accurate and has been fairly determined. Only OHC officials can examine, review, or correct your application. You may wait for years without ever hearing that they have a place for you. All you can do to ensure that they still know you're there is to bug them, and to increase your point rating by having more kids, living in a house which hydro or housing authorities will condemn, reducing your income, increasing your rent or getting yourself evicted by an expressway project.

The people who live on the east side of Wilkins Avenue find themselves about to be evicted. Ten days ago they all received the same letter from their new landlords, Fluxgold Investments Ltd. and Sam Lichtman Enterprises Ltd. The letter was to the point: "Take notice that we, as landlords of the above-noted property, demand that you vacate the said premises on or before the first day of July, 1969. You are hereby given notice to vacate the said premises on this the --- day of May, 1969."

The lawyer for the new owners, D. C. McTavish of Rose, Persiko and Arnold, told me he has no idea what the new owners of Wilkins Avenue intend to do with the street's 20 houses. But it looks very much like a street ready for town house renovations.*

Wilkins Avenue's frame row houses were built 70 or 80 years ago. Their brick false fronts were put on about 15 years ago. They are not in good condition, though the

---

*This has since proved to be the case.

houses apparently meet some or all of the city's minimum housing standards. Floors sag, wiring is limited, all kinds of small repairs are needed. Many of the tenants have done a lot of work themselves, but they consider the houses to be in bad shape. "If I took down the wallpaper I've put up, the house would fall down," one of them told me while several others agreed.

When they received their eviction notices, the people on the east side of Wilkins Avenue got together and decided to go to OHC as a group to request public housing. OHC officials were notified that they were coming and as soon as application forms had been filled out in the ordinary waiting room on the fifth floor Mrs. Betty Meredith, responsible for tenant selection in Toronto, came out to say that the waiting room wasn't the best place to talk; perhaps, she said, we could all go downstairs.

Downstairs proved to be a board room, carpeted, with luxury swivel armchairs, a large table and an easel made to have architects' sketches of beautiful high-rise OHC buildings pinned to it. With Mrs. Meredith came Eric J. Whaley, property manager for OHC.

Harry Robinson, minister of Little Trinity Church which is located a block from Wilkins Avenue, asked if he should introduce everyone. "Yes, that would be nice," said Mrs. Meredith, and the tone of the meeting was established.

The matter which Wilkins Avenue residents had come to discuss was whether OHC would provide them with accommodation on July 1 if they were unable to find suitable housing on the private market. This was discussed, but there were many sidetracks which also came up and which Mrs. Meredith and Mr. Whaley explored at some length.

The first of these sidetracks was the suggestion that people should have gone to the city rather than OHC to discuss their problems. Someone pointed out that the city has little to offer people who are about to be evicted; OHC is the only agency in Toronto with subsidized family public housing to offer.

More to the point, Mrs. Meredith assured everyone that their eviction notice was not as rigid as it sounded. She had been talking to the new owners' lawyer:

"He assured me that as long as we informed them as to the date of each person, you know, if we are looking after that particular application, that they [the landlords] would release them at any time and they [the tenants] would only be responsible for the rent for the number of days they were actually occupying the premises."

This was followed by another distraction; in what part of the city did people want their new OHC units? Then Mr. Whaley wanted to know if people had begun looking for housing on the private market. This produced an answer which explained simply the problem Wilkins Avenue tenants face. "We called one place last Thursday night on Donlands and Mortimer," said one lady. "She was asking $175 for an eight-room house. I asked her if she takes children; she said yes, but the rent went up immediately to $225 when I said eight children. And $225 a month I just couldn't manage."

A few minutes later, almost as if it was by accident, Mr. Whaley made the first direct statement on the matter the tenants had really come to discuss:

"Well, it would seem to me that with the cooperation of the new owners which we have already enlisted — the fact that we've been in contact with him — I'm sure that we can work out something that will ensure that nobody gets put out on the street." Nobody gets put out on the street: a commitment, but what did it mean?

Mrs. Meredith at this rather important point in the discussion produced a distraction in the form of the OHC home visitor; she wanted to arrange a visit to everyone on Wilkins Avenue. By this time Wilkins residents had seen that this meeting could deal with other small matters beside the main issue which they had come to discuss, and they came up with a number of these: one family has a notice that its hydro will be cut off June 17, a lady wondered if there was OHC housing near Maple where her husband works, someone else talked about having to get accommodation large enough that her invalid father could live with the family.

The meeting came back to the main subject with a question to Mr. Whaley: "I would like to know just exactly what is the assurance that you're giving here today; you said earlier that no one would be put out on the street; do I read that to mean that in a case where someone is unable to find suitable accommodation you're guaranteeing to provide them OHC accommodation? "

"We can't guarantee to provide OHC accommodation," Mr. Whaley replied, "because it all depends on what we have and when we have it. What we are guaranteeing is that we will work with the landlord to ensure that between he and ourselves that nobody gets put out on the street."

Nobody gets put out on the street: did that mean OHC would try in court to block any move to evict the tenants? That OHC would in fact guarantee last-resort housing? Or that it would arrange to have anyone about to be deposited on the street picked up and taken to the city's emergency housing hostel for women and children?

It wasn't clear; but there was an interruption, the question of the lady who wanted to be close to Maple came up again, and then Mr. Whaley politely brought the meeting to a close.

Discussing this meeting the next day, the Wilkins Avenue residents decided that they would give OHC a week to see what would happen. They will be meeting again this Thursday in Little Trinity Church to review the situation and to decide what to do next. It could be another group visit to OHC; it could be an attempt to have questions asked in the provincial legislature, it could be a move to stop the evictions.

Even though their first meeting produced only vague statements, it made its real point: Wilkins Avenue residents have established themselves as a group, are not begging but negotiating for public housing and are doing so in a highly-visible way. If they continue to deal with OHC as a group rather than going individually, they stand a good chance of getting the substance as well as the appearance of fair, concerned, impartial treatment from OHC and they will have demonstrated a new way of applying for public housing in Toronto.

* * *

Once OHC had recovered from the shock of encountering an organized group of tenant applicants for the first time, it quickly went about trying to break down the Wilkins group, and to impress upon its members the need for showing proper deference and humility in order to succeed at getting into public housing. Most of the Berkeley and Wilkins tenants were left dangling until the end of June or later, with no definite offer of housing from OHC. When they called to find out what progress their applications were making or to ask about vacant units they knew about in OHC projects, they received the usual treatment from corporation employees. Finally, when they decided that they should go as a group a second time to negotiate with OHC, because they were making so little progress, they brought the issue of how applicants must deal with OHC to a head. OHC officials refused to admit me or my tape recorder to the meeting; much more serious, they refused to allow John Sewell to attend the meeting as a lawyer acting for some of the Wilkins residents. At the meeting, with no outsiders present, they made it clear to the Berkeley-Wilkins people that they were endangering their chances of success by attracting publicity, by having newspapers writing about them, and by consorting with troublemakers like Sewell.

In a third article on the experiences of Berkeley-Wilkins residents, written after all were rehoused (most in OHC units), I discussed the way that OHC deals with its applicants, using the experiences of Berkeley-Wilkins residents to illustrate its practices.

What happens to public housing applicants

How does the Ontario Housing Corporation deal with the 11,000 families in Metro Toronto applying for its subsidized-rent public housing units? According to OHC, the corporation is diligent, efficient and fair. "Ontario housing will be allocated on the basis of greatest need and not on a first-come-first-served basis," says a small pamphlet used in OHC survey mailings. "Points are allowed for factors such as inadequacy of present accommodation, total income, rent paid as a percentage of income, notice to vacate for reasons other than cause, members of the family living apart through lack of accommodation and health conditions aggravated by present accommodation." Says a recent OHC report to Metro Council, "Allocation is made on the basis of the greatest number of points, taking into account the bedroom requirements and location preference."

OHC provides its tenants with better-quality housing at lower rents than they could obtain on the private market. No one knows that better than OHC's applicants, who are all too familiar with what kind of houses are available in downtown Toronto for $100 or $120 a month. The number of OHC low-rent units in Toronto is small; it is, of course, increasing, although the additions to the low-cost housing stock in the city made by OHC probably fall short of the reductions caused by demolition for new development and renovation for the town house market. But everyone, including OHC, agrees there is a serious shortage of decent low-cost housing.

What OHC's applicants come face to face with, however, is not just *what* OHC is doing; it is *how* OHC is doing it. OHC says it is straightforward, impartial and fair. To its applicants, it often seems just the opposite.

In the past eight weeks, I have observed, and sometimes participated in, the activities of the families who lived on the east side of Wilkins Avenue and on Berkeley Street who were trying to get into OHC housing. All had received eviction notices from their landlords in late May to leave by the end of June; almost all have children; some receive welfare and mothers' allowance. All but three or four of the families found it impossible to get decent housing they could afford on the private market. The families used all the means open to them of putting their situation before OHC. They phoned, they wrote letters, they had newspaper articles written about them, they went to OHC as a group twice, they picketed, and they contacted their member of the legislature, Mines Minister Allan Lawrence. By the middle of July, all the families had been offered OHC housing and most had accepted it.

You might think as a result they would have a favorable view of OHC. But they haven't. Their story had a happy ending; why has it left a sour taste in their mouths?

In the course of these last few weeks, they came to see OHC as refusing to tell them the truth, pretending that it didn't know what was going on in its own projects in Toronto, infringing their rights, and consciously or unconsciously drawing a clear, firm line between them as public housing applicants and other people.

They got this impression from OHC on major and minor matters both. Take small things like telephone calls. OHC has a policy that applicants who are offered housing are called about it and the phone call is followed by a letter. On this minor point, I witnessed a three-sided conversation between a Wilkins Avenue resident, the group's lawyer, John Sewell, and OHC's supervisor of tenant selection for Metro Toronto, Mrs. Betty Meredith. The OHC official said that the applicant had been phoned. When Mr. Sewell said that she hadn't, Mrs. Meredith said that she had no phone. When the applicant pointed out that she did indeed have a phone, Mrs. Meredith said then she was sure the phone call had been made. When the lady said that it hadn't, Mrs. Meredith then said that OHC didn't have the phone number.

It, was of course, a small matter. Mrs. Meredith has all sorts of applicants to deal with all the time; she could easily have gotten her facts wrong about this particular case. But she left no room for doubt. Mrs. Meredith was *certain* the call had been made; then *certain* that the lady had no phone; and then *certain* that OHC didn't have the phone number. If there was error, if there was confusion, apparently as far as she was concerned it could only be on the part of the applicant. But as far as the applicant was concerned, OHC had lied on a matter as trivial as a phone call.

A second incident concerned a rather more important matter. During the tense weeks of June and early July as the Wilkins-Berkeley applicants waited for letters from OHC offering them housing, they heard from friends about OHC housing that appeared to be vacant, or where construction had been completed but families had not yet moved in. Several times people phoned OHC to bring this to the corporation's attention and to ask if they could move in to the vacant units. Applicants who phoned were told either that work had not been completed on the project or that the official answering the phone had no information on the subject. Finally, in late June, a group of applicants went on a tour of a number of OHC projects nearing completion in Toronto to see if any of them were ready for occupancy. At the Blake Street project, they found row houses which appeared to be completed and ready for families to move in. One door happened to be unlocked, and with a reporter from the *Toronto Star* they went inside and had a look. The walls were painted, the water and electricity were turned on, and everything that they could see inside was complete except for the installation of the refrigerator and stove. Grass and shrubs had been planted in the back yard, but there was no grass at the front and the construction fence had not been taken down. One of the applicants phoned OHC that day and was told that these units were not completed because there was no grass on the front lawns. The next day a group of people took rakes and grass seed and planted grass in front of some of the houses. Then they phoned OHC to say that some of the units now had grass at the front and to ask if they could now be occupied. The officials they spoke to on the phone could only repeat that the houses were not completed. What conclusion could they draw? It seemed clear that the officials they talked to on the phone were prepared to say anything and to tell them nothing. There might well have been several good reasons why the houses could not yet be occupied; for instance, these applicants might have been in less urgent need than the people to whom OHC was planning to offer the houses. But they were given no information except that the houses were not complete, information which did not correspond to what they could see with their own eyes.

A third incident occurred in mid-June. It happened because Wilkins and Berkeley residents regarded themselves not as petitioners to OHC but as citizens demanding a service which the Ontario government has agreed should be provided for its citizens. They were not asking for a favor, in their view; they were demanding what should be their right.

When their eviction notices first arrived, they organized themselves as a group and went to OHC to see what it was prepared to do. With them at the meeting which took place in OHC's head office were Mr. Sewell and Harry Robinson, minister of the nearby Little Trinity Church. I also accompanied them and later wrote an article based on the tape recording I made of the meeting. OHC officials were aware that I was present with my tape recorder and did not appear pleased about it, but chose not to object. The commitment which the Berkeley-Wilkins residents were given by OHC implicitly recognized their right to housing; one way or another, they were told, OHC will ensure that you are not put out on the street.

But almost three weeks later, little visible progress had been made by OHC, and Berkeley-Wilkins applicants were having difficulty obtaining any information about what OHC was doing and what their chances were of getting public housing. They decided to go again as a group to OHC's head office. Mr. Sewell was asked to accompany them as their counsel; I was invited to go with my tape recorder. I was barred from the meeting by Eric Whaley, OHC deputy managing director, and other OHC officials. I thought this was regrettable but not surprising. Very few serious negotiations ever take place in front of newspaper writers. But at the same time Mr. Sewell also was barred. He objected vehemently, telling Mr. Whaley, that he was a lawyer and he was there as counsel for OHC's applicants. Mr. Whaley was not left with any doubts on this score. "Is he representing you? " he asked one of the residents. "Yes, he is," was the reply.

Mr. Whaley cited two reasons for keeping Mr. Sewell out of the meeting and refusing to allow it to continue if he was present. He said that Mr. Sewell's presence would make it a public meeting, although Mr. Sewell said he was acting not as a member of the public but as an agent of the applicants. Mr. Whaley's other reason was that he wanted no tape recorders at the meeting. Mr. Sewell pointed out that he was a lawyer, not a tape recorder.

Why should OHC have found so objectionable the idea that the Berkeley-Wilkins applicants should want to have a lawyer with them? No doubt it was partly that the previous meeting had led OHC to associate lawyers with press and press with articles about them in the newspapers.

Whatever its reasons, these applicants found OHC treating them as mere petitioners, asking favors; people in such a position should not have a lawyer at their side. Such people do not have a right to public housing; rather, it is bestowed on them on the basis of a public agency's judgment of their worthiness.

As a result of this second meeting, many of the Berkeley-Wilkins applicants got the impression from OHC that they have a special status as people who want public housing. Their status is not to demand and receive fair treatment; to ask (as they had) for details of the number of points each family had been allocated and for information on where they stood on the waiting list for homes so they had a reasonable idea of what their chances were. Instead, they were asking for a special privilege and OHC clearly thought that all they were supposed to do was request that favor and wait quietly to see if it was granted.

Their sense of special status was reinforced in another encounter between OHC and some of the Berkeley-Wilkins applicants. This took place at the official opening June 27 of the first of OHC's new high-rise apartments in St. James Town. These are low-rental units mainly for couples and families with older children (although there appear to be a number of small children living in the building now). There were perhaps 250 people present at the opening. Among them were mayors, cabinet ministers, social agency luminaries, members of OHC's board of directors, planners, OHC and city officials, and municipal politicians galore. Missing from this list of invited guests was one obvious group: representatives of the 11,000 families on OHC's waiting list, some of whom would be living in this new building. The omission was corrected by half a dozen of OHC's Berkeley Street applicants who went to the opening uninvited. As the official speeches were made, they stood on the other side of the street and held up signs: "OHC Unfair to Applicants — Why can't we get into Blake Street? " and "OHC do not keep their promises to applicants."

After the opening, those present were invited to go on tours to see the apartments and the building's facilities. Two guards, apparently hired especially for the occasion, stood holding the doors open as people filed in.

One of the Berkeley Street applicants was about to go through the door when a guard stopped her. "It's by invitation," he said.

Another applicant who had already been stopped explained: "It's for all the big officials."

As the applicants waited, other people filed through the door. The guards did not ask anyone to show his invitation; people were sorted out solely on the basis of their appearance. Anyone who looked like a lady alderman or a social worker was let in without question; the women who did not were assumed to be uninvited.

The crowd outside the building got smaller and smaller until it was made up only of Berkeley Street applicants and some of the people who lived in the old houses across the street from the new building and who decided that they would like to have a look, too. Those outside peered in at those inside waiting for their tours to begin. Those inside looked, rather uneasily, at those outside.

Perhaps it had seemed administratively impossible to OHC for it to invite some or all of its applicants to this official opening. Perhaps the idea never occurred to OHC. But, once some applicants were there, OHC's officials might well have tried to make these uninvited guests, whose interest in OHC was certainly as great as that of most of the other people present, feel as welcome as anyone else.

Many of the invited guests saw what was happening. Only one protested, a planner from the Toronto Planning Board, but then he had told me earlier that he had no invitation either.

In the end, Allan Lawrence, member of the legislature for the riding which includes Berkeley Street and St. James Town, arranged for the applicants to go through the building. They were taken on a separate but equal tour by themselves.

All of these experiences leave these people with the conviction that OHC is an agency that will never tell them what is going on, which sometimes misleads and sometimes lies, and which attributes to them special status of inferiority on the grounds that they are public housing applicants.

Their normal rights to open and honest dealings with government agencies, to fair treatment, to information, to whatever legal advice and assistance they wish, to respect and dignity, are suspended insofar as their dealings with OHC are concerned.

No doubt OHC's management and officials will find it hard to see why these applicants have formed this impression. They probably feel that life is full of misunderstandings about phone calls, and of parties to which only some are admitted. This doesn't lead most people to the impression that everyone else is unfair, dishonest, or denying the rights of fellow citizens. OHC may find it hard to see why its applicants should come to conclusions of this kind.

But OHC's dominant reaction will probably be that the Berkeley-Wilkins people who applied for OHC housing, of all the 11,000 families on OHC's waiting list, have the least to complain about. After all, the story has a happy ending: all were offered, and most accepted, OHC housing.

But that misses the point. The issue is not *what* OHC did in this case; it is *how* OHC did it. It is that in doing something which the applicants found extremely valuable, OHC acted in ways which degrade and demean exactly the people that it is supposed to be serving.

* * *

There is nothing special or unusual about what happened to the Berkeley-Wilkins tenants when they applied to OHC for public housing. Their experiences are not extreme; the examples used in the article are not specially chosen. This is what happens to the average public housing applicant.

And experiences of this kind are by no means limited to public housing agencies. All government agencies, and government itself, treat most people, and especially working-class people, in much the same way. Government manpower offices, welfare departments, workmen's compensation boards, children's aid societies, the police, city government urban renewal agencies – the list goes on and on. There is always the same assumption of the inferiority of the person being served, the same denial of rights and of dignity, the same willingness to mislead and to lie if it is convenient, the same refusal to treat people in a just, equitable way. The encounter between the Ontario Housing Corporation and twenty families from Berkeley and Wilkins illustrates the typical conduct of government. It is no different from the conduct of the Toronto Board of Education dealing with the residents of the Cornwall-

Oak area and the people whose children would attend the new school. The facts change from case to case, but the story seems to be always much the same.

Chapter Six
Developers: Public and Private

Toronto is in a period of rapid physical growth. Land development and redevelopment is being managed (perhaps non-managed would be a better term) during this period by the governments and public agencies of the Toronto area in ways which are apparently very acceptable and highly profitable to real estate and development interests. One other consequence of these policies is that virtually every residential area of the city is under some kind of development pressure, either from high-rise apartment developers, or from subway and expressway builders, airport authorities, road wideners and improvers, university and school board expropriators, or town house renovators. Of course the total amount of land actually used for all these purposes in the course of a year is not that great in comparison to the size of the city, but the impact of these changes is very widely felt. This is partly because every change takes five or ten or fifteen years in coming, a long period of time during which everyone in the area actually involved and in the neighboring areas is directly affected. It is also because development policies are uncertain, and no one can ever be sure exactly where something is really going to happen. In such a simple matter as the people who live in houses on the edge of an existing school, for instance, expansion of the school site (which happens often enough to be possible for almost every existing school) is likely to take place in one direction only, but since no one knows which direction the school administration will choose, people in all four directions feel uncertain. For every piece of land where a new high-rise apartment is actually built, there may be ten, perhaps twenty, areas where speculators and developers make inquiries, perhaps buy up a few properties, and talk to people about options. Residents in all ten or twenty areas feel the pressure.

Perhaps the most interesting fact about the many private businesses and public authorities who act as land developers is that there is a single technique of land development which is used by everyone, from the most unscrupulous money-hungry developer to the most respectable public institution. The three articles in this chapter document the activities of three land developers: Meridian Property Management, the University of Toronto, and the U of T's Students' Administrative Council. Meridian is one of the three or four largest and most respectable development firms in Toronto. It has built high-rise apartments in both downtown and suburban areas. The University of Toronto has been involved in expanding its central-city campus at a very fast rate for the last 15 or 20 years. The university's student organization has never actually acted as a land developer, but it had ambitions to build student residences to show the U of T how well the job could be done. It got as far as acquiring land for its proposed residence and hiring architects who drew up detailed plans for the building; this and the decision the students' organization made about their site were enough to illustrate how similar their land development techniques were to those of every other land developer.

The area south of the St. James Town apartment complex is immediately to the west of the Don Vale urban renewal area. In plans prepared by city planners in 1963 and 1965, the area was recommended for retention as medium-density residential. Most of the houses, according to the city's planners in 1963 and to an independent group of Metro planners in 1965, were in good enough condition that they warranted preservation and rehabilitation. In the summer of 1968, however, the planners' proposals were amended by City Council and the city's new official plan designated south of St. James Town for eventual high-density residential development. This change took place after speculators and developers, including Meridian, had begun to buy property and to take up options in the neighborhood.

In the past, downtown areas have been redeveloped with very little political activity on the part of local residents and property owners. In the St. James Town project, the largest private redevelopment project undertaken so far in Toronto, there was some resistance from residents. South of St. James Town, a residents' association was set up in early 1969 by local people with help from some outside community organizers. The new group began to discuss the situation they faced; it tried to find out as much as possible about the facts of their circumstances; and it decided that it would attempt to influence the nature of any project for the area. Part of the process of finding out what was going on involved talking to the firm with major interests there, and the principal owner of Meridian, Philip Roth, attended a public meeting where he was questioned. I wrote an article about what was said at that meeting.

August 15, 1969

The problems and policies of a land developer

Last week about 75 residents of the area south of St. James Town went to a meeting where they hoped to learn what the future of their area will be. Scheduled to speak at the meeting were officials of Meridian Property Management Ltd., which was involved in the St. James Town redevelopment and which has bought many of the old houses immediately to the south, between Parliament and Sherbourne Streets, from Wellesley Street on the north to Carlton Street on the south.

Philip Roth, one of the directors of the firm, told residents at the meeting that he has no firm ideas about the long-term future of this area. He expects that at some time Meridian will approach the city with a detailed development proposal and a request for rezoning. But he said that he had no idea when that might happen. And when residents asked what the proposed redevelopment would be, whether it would be apartments for families with children, low-rent housing, senior citizens' accommodation, or more of what was built in St. James Town, Mr. Roth said that at this point he and his firm don't know.

Since Mr. Roth had nothing definite to say about the long-term future, residents turned to the more immediate matter of what is going to happen in the interim period before redevelopment while the existing houses still stand. On this subject, Mr. Roth was open and frank about his firm's policies. He explained that it is involved in what is essentially a holding operation. It has bought many of the houses in the area, is picking up options before they expire, and is renting these properties out to tenants for the time being. Mr. Roth explained that Meridian's practices in the management of these properties stem from what it sees as its immediate economic interests. Its main concern is with the land on which the houses stand. It expects that before long the houses will be torn down.

"I am putting the least possible money into these houses," said Mr. Roth. "I do not have money to put back into them. Renting them is not a money-making business for us. So if a tenant happens to break a sink, he may find that I'm not the best landlord in the world."

Of course, Meridian is legally obliged to keep the houses up to the minimum housing standards bylaw enforced across the city. Doing this minimum legal level of maintenance makes it possible for tenants to continue living in the houses and puts off at least temporarily another reduction in the city's low-cost housing stock.

For Meridian this practice has the intended effect of minimizing its losses during the period before redevelopment. And it is exactly that which Mr. Roth, as a businessman, is concerned about. It also has some other effects and it was these that Mr. Roth heard about from people at the meeting. It is not in the interest of Meridian to do large-scale repair work or to continue with some kinds of maintenance, but the absence of this work makes a difference in the area which local people notice. One woman at the meeting cited a house next to hers where a lovely back garden now has grass four feet high. Broken cellar windows are left for a long time before they're fixed. Slowly, as the absence of this repair and maintenance work makes itself felt, the physical condition of the area deteriorates.

.It was clear from what Mr. Roth said that Meridian's intentions are focussed not on this deterioration, but on longer-term matters, on the eventual redevelopment, on minimizing the costs of the properties it owns until the time when redevelopment is economically feasible and permission has been obtained from the city, and on minimizing the costs of acquiring the remaining houses in the area. The deterioration, the condition of existing houses, is an unintended but natural result of Meridian following its economic interest.

This situation concerned residents. But what worried them more were the effects of another property management practice of Meridian's which Mr. Roth explained. Some of the houses it owns are larger than single-family homes, larger than five or six rooms. These are big enough for more than one family to live in separate flats or for rooms to be rented out individually to roomers. Meridian's practice regarding these houses is to rent them out to single individuals. The firm does not operate rooming houses, Mr. Roth said, and it has no desire to get involved in renting out individual rooms or flats. What Meridian does is find one principal tenant who pays $130 or $150 a month and rents an entire house for that price. Meridian places one condition on tenancy: that the tenant agree to maintain the house so that it meets the city's housing standards bylaw. No other conditions or restrictions are placed by Meridian on these tenants or on the people who rent the single-family houses it owns. "I am not concerned with what our tenants do," Mr. Roth said. "They are free to do what they want. We don't check back continuously on what they are doing."

This practice deals simply and efficiently with the problem which these larger houses pose for Meridian. They are rented; they produce a relatively small but steady revenue, and the firm does not have to worry about the constant stream of minor maintenance and repair work required to keep the houses up to standard. It achieves its intended effect of minimizing the firm's losses in the interim period.

This practice has, however, other consequences. What apparently has happened south of St. James Town is that many of these larger houses have been rented by tenants who then act as middlemen. Often the middlemen do not live in the houses they rent. Instead they rent them out in flats or rooms, earning revenue far higher than the rent they pay Meridian. One of the sub-tenants in a house rented by a middleman told me that he has been paying $100 a month for a small flat on the main floor. A woman upstairs, he said, pays $150. Altogether the house is producing close to $300 a month. A Meridian official told me that the house is rented by the firm for $150. I was also told by a Meridian official that one man rents 20 houses from the firm in the south of St. James Town area. If the tenant clears $250 a month from each house that he rents for $150, an assumption which is reasonable in the light of the rental value of the large houses in the area, he is making $2,000 a month. And the $2,000 represents all or part of the difference between the rents that the owner of the house is charging and the rents which the people who live in them are paying.

People at the meeting pointed out some of the conditions which this arrangement produces. One woman mentioned the people who live in a small flat and pay $150 a month in the house next to hers. "There are cockroaches popping out of their toaster; it's that bad," she said.

Sub-tenants are discouraged from repairing and maintaining their flats and rooms because they have no idea of when they are going to move. None has a lease; all are on a weekly or monthly basis and can be thrown out with that much notice.

Moreover, some of the middlemen make a practice of moving their sub-tenants every two months or so, evicting them from one house but offering them accommodation in another. All that the sub-tenants know for sure is that they won't be living in any one place for long, so of course they have no motive to do minor repairs or even to paint.

Many of the middlemen do their best to ensure that their tenants do not ask them to do repairs or maintenance work. Some middlemen refuse to give their sub-tenants a phone number or an address where they can be contacted. They are available only when they collect the rent and sub-tenants know very well that if they complain on rent day or request that repairs be made they run the risk of having their landlord hand their rent back and kick them out the same day.

The result is that sub-tenants of these middlemen have no incentive to care or worry. If some people have rowdy parties or leave their garbage on the front lawn, there is no one for other sub-tenants to complain to and no prospect that the middleman-landlord will do anything anyway.

The consequence of this arrangement is that the physical conditions in the area deteriorate further. In addition, long-time residents begin to feel harassed and to give up hope that their house or their street can be saved. They see their neighborhood going downhill right in front of their eyes.

Meridian certainly has no intention of harassing anyone or of making it difficult for people living in houses it owns to contact the person they have rented from, or of not keeping the houses up to the city's standards. Meridian is a development firm; it wants to develop. It is also a business; it wants to minimize its losses pending redevelopment. In the circumstances in which it must operate, its economic interest leads it to actions which are the most sensible and have the desired consequences for the firm. Yet at the same time, even though it clearly has no intention of doing so, its actions are having other effects as well which are not so desirable. It is these other unintended effects that the people at last week's meeting were concerned about. They, too, are interested in an eventual redevelopment scheme for the area, but they are worried about what is going to happen between now and the day that large-scale demolition begins.

* * *

It is interesting to put side by side with the article on the south of St. James Town area an article about the activities of the University of Toronto in a residential area to the north-west of its present downtown campus.

September 15, 1969

The University of Toronto as a land developer

"She's been told for years now that they're going to need her property," said Walt Zmud, one of the members of the executive committee of the Huron-Sussex Residents' Association at a meeting last Thursday. "We went down to visit her the other night, and you know the usual story: they visit her every six months, and say 'We're going to be needing your property.' They give her a price, which she turns down. And then, six months later, after having said that they're going to need the property immediately, they come back with another offer, another go-around, the same thing."

The technique Mr. Zmud was describing sounds just like the usual practice of speculators and developers who are trying to assemble property.

"You know the house next door to that one," added Miss Gertrude Ross, another member of the executive committee. "Sillcoxes owned that house and they kept it beautifully. You know the look of it now. They just let it go down and down and down; it's awful. And it was beautiful."

This is a familiar pattern. People who see their neighborhood running down in front of their eyes are easily persuaded to sell their homes even if they would really rather stay where they are. Houses that are sold are then rented to tenants who do not maintain them and who often cause trouble for remaining long-time residents. Members of the Huron-Sussex association have experienced this too: "A good example," said one resident, "is down here on Spadina just north of Sussex. They had people there who were very responsible." They left and kids moved in. "And the kids have really run the place down."

Another technique used by developers is to tear down houses that have not been repaired for some time, leaving vacant lots between long-time residents who have not yet sold. This the executive committee of the Huron-Sussex group has also seen. "I suppose they get a price for wrecking them," said one resident, "and find that it's less than fixing them up, and they leave the vacant lots sitting there. You can see this on Huron Street."

The people at last Thursday's meeting were quite aware that they were describing what very often happens in older residential areas. In their case, however, the purchaser whose practices they were complaining about is not a developer. It is, in fact, about as far from a developer as you could ever hope to get. The people from the Huron-Sussex association were complaining about the University of Toronto.

The U of T's downtown campus stands just south and east of the Huron-Sussex area. Immediately to the north is the Ontario College of Education. In between the two institutions are about 140 houses, on three quiet residential streets: Huron, Sussex, and Washington. Spadina Avenue is the western boundary of their neighborhood. Perhaps 300 families live in these houses, some of them students, some young couples, some long-established residents, middle-class and working-class side by side.

The Huron-Sussex Residents' Association was set up four months ago in response to rumors of imminent demolition of the entire area for use by OCE and the U of T. Its members are a cross-section of residents, and there are at least as many tenants as homeowners involved.

The situation in which they find themselves has been developing over the last several years. In 1961 U of T published a master building plan for its downtown campus covering the period to 1970 and providing for accommodation for about 23,000 students. This plan indicated clearly that, apart from what looked like a reasonably small expansion of OCE, the houses in the Huron-Sussex area would be left standing. A small descriptive leaflet, circulated at the time the plan was published, is reasonably definite in its projections. "The model is not precise in every detail, for changes are rapid and frequent. But, in general, the model provides a good illustration of how a great development plan is being implemented." In a speech that year, U of T president Claude Bissell said on the question of the geographical boundaries of university expansion: "Given our position in the centre of the city, there are obvious limits beyond which we cannot go, and by 1970 we shall have reached those limits." The plan and statements of this kind taken together indicated reasonable certainty to people in the Huron-Sussex area that the university would not be expanding as far as their small, pleasant neighborhood.

By 1967, however, the situation had changed considerably. Letters were sent to some property owners on the north side of Sussex between Huron and Spadina. One of these letters, said by university officials to be typical, stated: "It is necessary for us to ask you to consider the sale of these lands to the university." And, just in case the recipient of the letter wasn't in a selling mood, the university went on to give a none-too-gentle hint of what might happen if he did not sell: "The University of Toronto has under law the power to expropriate lands, subject to authorization by a county court judge, but it is to be hoped that we can reach agreement for a purchase of the lands without recourse to such action."

New university plans have been busy taking back Dr. Bissell's confident statement about reaching a ceiling on physical size as well as on enrolment. "Holding at the above enrolment," says one plan, "in no way assumes that floor space and land needs will also be held. On the contrary, space needs of all kinds will continue to rise."

One of the areas chosen by the university for expansion is that where members of the Huron-Sussex association now live. A university plan dated December 1968 proposes for their blocks a very large expansion for OCE, a building described as "parking for 600 cars with high-rise above," and a third building named Walker Hall which university officials have told residents is not yet designated for any particular use.

These plans apparently have been made by the U of T with no detailed consultations with either city planners or city politicians. Association members have been told that the city usually becomes involved only at a very late stage when the U of T makes specific requests for zoning changes, new services and so on.

What concerns residents most of all, however, is the fact that they have had nothing whatsoever to say in the formulation of these plans, even though it is they who will be evicted if the plan is to be implemented and even though, in many cases, it is they who own the properties where the university is confidently locating its new, vaguely-described buildings.

The association's executive has had meetings with university officials, and it has been made very clear to them that this is a state of affairs which the university has no intention of changing. University vice-president A. G. Rankin told them at one of these meetings: "You cannot tell the Board of Governors of the university how to operate. We are not prepared to allow you to take part in the planning of this area."

This extraordinarily heavy-handed comment was included verbatim in minutes of the meeting taken by association members. Mr. Rankin corrected some other parts of this record, but apparently regarded this as an accurate account of what he said.

How, in fact, does the university operate? Ron Thom, member of the Huron-Sussex executive and a planner for Trent University for the past six years, said: "We have realized that they have literally, not virtually but literally, no planning apparatus right now." The university has a planning department, said Mr. Thom, but it is staffed not by planners but by engineers.

Another member of the executive, architect Stan Benjamin, said they had discovered that the university has no fixed plan for its future expansion. As an example, he cited a refrigeration plant which the university is planning to build. Its location has, he said, been changed at least twice in recent plans.

Concerned as they are about the university's planning, the association's executive is even more worried about its property buying and management practices. So far, the U of T has bought 56 of the 143 properties in their area. These have been assembled slowly over the course of several years. Once purchased, they are rented by an agency retained by the university. They are usually not well maintained and often they are demolished long before any new building takes place on the site.

Complaints about vacant lots have produced the association's only achievement to date: the university sodded one vacant lot on the south-west corner of Washington and Huron.

Often houses which the university purchases are taken out of the housing market altogether, either by demolition or by using them as office space. Sometimes they are simply left vacant. Miss Ross cited a house on the corner of Washington and Spadina which, she said, has been empty for more than two years. "The windows are out . . . there's been a top window open all the time, through winter, spring and summer, and a window on the second floor has been open, and it sits there."

"The reason this has sat empty," a resident explained, "is that it has been allocated to university use and the faculty, as I understand it, that it has been allocated to hasn't bothered to use it. So there it sits, with its air conditioners and everything; and it was very nice, it was a good house at one time."

There have been many complaints in the past from residents of surrounding areas about the U of T's practices, but these have had no impact on the university's activities. And usually, in fact, it has had little difficulty persuading residents that there was nothing for them to do but move when the university said it has to expand in their direction.

Planner Ron Thom said at last week's meeting, referring to his experience working at Trent: "I have more trouble moving a farmer off his potato patch than these people are having moving out 800 people."

As residents of the Huron-Sussex area learn more about the university's plans and practices, however, their attitude is hardening. Mr. Zmud said that before he became involved he had been prepared to accommodate himself to the university's plans once he had definite information on what these were. Now, he said, "I'm prepared to say, well, to hell with you, university, unless you demonstrate to me that you really absolutely need this land which is still a community." Faced with that kind of attitude from Huron-Sussex residents, university officials may find that they either do their planning for that area with city planners and local residents or they will learn from hard experience that people are not prepared to go as quietly as they have in the past.

* * *

The U of T's Students' Administrative Council has never actually carried out a land development. It has, nevertheless, learned some of the essential techniques of development from its experience in 1968 trying to build a model student residence. The site which happened to be chosen for this residence was in the Kensington urban renewal area which is just to the west and the south of the university's downtown campus.

September 29, 1969

Students as land developers

"I wish to assure you," said the letter written a year ago for Premier John Robarts to the president of the Kensington Area Residents' Association, "that no final decision will be made on this matter without adequate discussion with you and representatives of your organization."

The matter referred to in the letter written by Mr. Robarts' executive officer was a parcel of 52,000 square feet of land fronting on College Street between Lippincott Street and Bellevue Avenue in the Kensington area. This land had been bought in the spring of 1968 by the University of Toronto apparently in trust for the provincial government and using a special $525,000 treasury grant to pay for it. At that time, the land was intended for a students' residence to be built not by the U of T but by the Students' Administrative Council (SAC).

Now, a year later, the land is in the hands of Toronto's Board of Education and the board has said that it intends to expropriate some houses and build a school on the larger site.

A block plan prepared by the neighborhood's residents proposing a comprehensive redevelopment of the interior of the block by a locally-based, limited-dividend corporation has proved futile.

There is an interesting story involved in how SAC, the U of T, the Board of Education and the provincial government got together to make this land sale, including an interesting set of minutes from secret SAC meetings discussing its building project and the Kensington residents.

Kensington is one of Toronto's current urban renewal planning areas and, along with a long-established businessmen's association, the community has a residents' association. In September, 1968, City Council established the Kensington Urban Renewal Committee with Controller Margaret Campbell as its chairman and the two aldermen of the ward and representatives of the local associations as its members. City Council delegated to the committee the power to supervise in detail the preparation of an urban renewal plan.

As a background to the planning which has been going on in Kensington, there is an important commitment regarding citizen participation made in October, 1967, on behalf of the provincial government by Minister of Correctional Services Allan Grossman who is also the MPP for the constituency which includes Kensington.

Mr. Grossman, who said last week that he was "most proud" to have been able to have brought about this commitment, conveyed to Kensington residents a formal agreement from the government not to participate in the implementation of any future urban renewal schemes which had not been prepared with the detailed participation of local residents. Mr. Grossman, when he read the commitment at a public meeting in the area in 1967, went on to spell out his interpretation of it. "This means in simple terms," he said, "that you are going to have a great deal to say about how your district is going to be developed. The Ontario government is going to refuse to participate in any kind of urban redevelopment until it is satisfied that the people in the district not only know what's going on but that they will be represented on the committee which makes the decision – and that they'll be in agreement with it."

The residents' association and the URC interpreted this commitment to mean that the provincial government wanted to ensure that the interests and views of local people were fully protected and represented in the decisions about the future of their area.

When, in the spring of 1968, the province financed a land deal intended to give SAC a site for a students' residence they could build themselves, the Kensington residents' association executive became seriously worried that the provincial government might not be prepared to ensure that residents have a say in the development of a specific redevelopment project, even though this building and the use it would make of extremely scarce vacant land would have substantial effects on the rest of the area and the urban renewal plan. But the letter from Mr. Robarts promising "adequate discussion" was interpreted as a reasonable guarantee that this would not happen.

The Kensington residents might also have felt less need to worry because they were dealing with university students regarding this land, and of course there is no group which professes a more sincere commitment to decentralized decision-making and participation by people in decisions which affect their lives. This was expressed concretely in a decision taken by SAC that a local community should have a veto over any redevelopment project within its boundaries. In a letter to U of T vice-president A. G. Rankin, the then SAC president, Steven Langdon, spelled out that this motion was passed by SAC with specific reference to Kensington. "This is the firmest indication I can offer," wrote Mr. Langdon, "of the good intentions of SAC in its development planning for anything within the Kensington Area Residents' Association boundaries."

Beginning in about mid-1968 two planning efforts, both centred on the land purchased with provincial money and held by the U of T, got under way. One of these was the work of the urban renewal committee and the residents' association through discussions with developers and a series of block meetings with residents of the College-Lippincott-Bellevue block where the vacant land is located. After considering the needs of the area, and the available alternatives, the urban renewal committee proposed for discussion a scheme for a multi-use redevelopment of the interior of the block by a limited-dividend corporation owned by the present owners of land in the block. The corporation, which would be able to borrow money at specially low interest rates under the National Housing Act, would hire a builder to put up a development which could include student accommodation, housing for nurses, interns and possibly some non-acutely ill patients from Toronto Western Hospital, some residential accommodation, a local city hall to house certain city services and a rebuilt, or new, firehall. There was also consideration of the need for more school facilities in the area, and the urban renewal committee proposed that the idea of a decentralized community school be explored for Kensington rather than having a new school or an addition on an existing school automatically put up.

After discussions took place with several builder-developers, an agreement was made with Cadillac Development Corporation Ltd. under which Cadillac drew up plans for the proposed development in exchange for a commitment in principle that it would build the project if satisfactory agreements could be reached with all concerned.

When these plans were ready, block meetings were held in January, February and March with residents to discuss these proposals and alternatives. Those at the meetings had many criticisms and suggestions to make of the original plans, but the general impression left by the detailed minutes of the meeting and confirmed by people who attended the meetings is that agreement among most, if not all, of the block's residents on a modified scheme looked possible.

SAC was informed about these plans by the Kensington Urban Renewal Committee. Although everyone from the area and from the university kept repeating his desire to coordinate planning activities, in fact SAC was simultaneously developing (apparently at a cost of about $75,000) its own detailed plans for a high-rise students' residence on the vacant lot in the centre of this block.

In a letter to the urban renewal committee on February 13, Mr. Langdon spelled out the kind of development the students had in mind. But there was no hint in his letter that SAC had detailed plans drawn up or that it was going ahead independently trying to finance the project.

Yet apparently this was happening. In February, according to Ed Clarke, secretary of the urban renewal committee, the architect retained by the students published detailed plans for the students' residence in a professional journal. Until this happened, no one in Kensington had any inkling that these plans existed. SAC was also apparently trying to obtain Central Mortgage and Housing Corporation funds to finance its project, but got nowhere. CMHC was no doubt aware that the project fell within an area where CMHC was contributing to the cost of an overall urban renewal plan.

SAC, blocked in its attempt to finance its residence, also realized that it would encounter enormous opposition if it tried to push through its scheme for a high-rise students' residence providing no substantial facilities for the area. SAC had hired Brian Levitt, until this spring a U of T student and now an employee of the university's administration, to investigate the situation for it. Mr. Levitt held discussions with Kensington residents and urban renewal committee members and learned about the proposals which residents had developed for the block. On May 27, Mr. Levitt was reporting to a secret SAC meeting on the residents' plans. Students at the meeting heard that there was no doubt that the residents' association would oppose the students' plan.

Their reaction was *not* to explore how their plans might be modified so as to suit residents. SAC's employee gave an account of the Kensington situation which reported that a small group had taken firm control of the residents' association, and that the association was completely unrepresentative of the ordinary people. Mr. Levitt sounded just like every city politician complaining about trouble-making and unrepresentative residents' associations. In fact he suggested that the Kensington situation was much worse than that; he said that the active members of the residents' association were all controlled by one individual, and he went on to suggest that this individual might be a secret agent for developers. The reaction of SAC members to this report was not to wonder if there was more to the story than they were hearing, but rather to suggest that SAC might hire its own community organizers to agitate in Kensington against the residents' association and to try to break down its "hold" on the neighborhood. No one seemed to think that ordinary Kensington residents would object to SAC putting up the first high-rise building in Kensington, in the middle of a block with houses on three sides of it, when vacant land was in short supply and other institutions in the area (particularly the hospital and the technical college) were likely to want to expand.

By May 27, however, SAC was apparently well into its preparations to give up its project, have the land sold, and to recover the money it had spent planning. Its minutes suggest that SAC had been in contact with the Board of Education and that the board was ready to buy the land for about $600,000.

Mr. Levitt said that the residents' association would vigorously object if it learned that SAC was considering selling its lands to the board because residents were hoping that the board would consider a decentralized community school and did not want to see scarce vacant land used for a school without considering all the competing demands for it.

It is interesting to note that SAC paid no attention to residents' proposals for decentralizing schools in Kensington. The minutes of the secret meeting describe its reaction to Mr. Levitt's description of the proposal as "snorts and ha's."

SAC knew that it needed the consent and cooperation of the provincial government if it were to be able to sell this land to the Board of Education. "We will be finished," say the minutes of a secret SAC meeting June 1, "if (Education Minister William) Davis does not say that it is all right to sell the land." On the morning of June 19, members of the urban renewal committee were later told, the land was released for sale. By the end of the afternoon it had been purchased by the Toronto Board of Education. Apparently Mr. Davis' consent to the sale had been obtained by SAC.

The dismay and anger of members of the Kensington residents' association executive when they learned of this land deal was reported in the press at the time. They suspected, though they had no documentary proof at that time, that the students, the province, the university and the Board of Education had cooked up a deal behind their backs.

Why this should have been done has not been explained. Nor has SAC explained what happened to its commitment to local residents that they would have a veto over any development proposal, a commitment which seemed to evaporate when SAC realized that residents would probably oppose the plans drawn up by SAC's architects. More important, no one has explained what has happened to the provincial government's commitment that residents would have a real say in what happens in their area.

Last week Mr. Grossman explained to me that the commitment really was a very limited one and applied only when the province is faced with the choice of approving or not approving a completed urban renewal plan. But Mr. Robarts, in his letter concerning this piece of land written a year ago, went further than that, promising "no final decision" without "adequate discussion."

Nor has the Board of Education explained why it needed to buy land for a school in Kensington. Residents know well that the board obtained a large tract of land when homes were expropriated as part of the Alexandra Park urban renewal project next to Ryerson Public School. The urban renewal plan called for an addition to Ryerson and this could serve Kensington, but though the board has owned the land for about two years, the addition has not been built.

It is not surprising that people should question the

real value of the provincial government's commitment that local planning decisions for Kensington should be taken not at secret meetings by public officials and politicians but by open discussion where the people most affected have a real say in what is done.

* * *

Following the publication of the article on the University of Toronto's land development policies, the *Globe and Mail* assigned one of its writers to do a long piece on university planning and building policies. The article was much more comprehensive in its scope than my piece had been, but its description of the university's activities was much the same. These articles appeared at the same time as news stories which reported that the university for some time had not been paying municipal taxes on land it owned which was not being used directly for educational purposes, land like the houses in the Huron-Sussex area which are being rented. Gradually the question of the U of T and its relationship to the city and to people in surrounding areas became one which came up frequently in the news, and the university apparently decided that it could no longer afford to ignore the sniping. A counter-attack was launched with a letter to the editor of the *Globe* from U of T's president, Claude Bissell, saying that the university was in fact extremely responsible in its land development policies. University officials including Dr. Bissell agreed to attend a public meeting of the Huron-Sussex association in mid-December to explain the university's policies. Though this meeting was scheduled specially so that Bissell could attend, he did not appear. Various other university officials, however, used the opportunity to explain how the university was expanding quickly and to make the automatic (and indefensible) assumption that expansion meant using more land from the surrounding area instead of, for instance using existing university land more intensively or decentralizing more of the university's activities. They did not explain the fact (revealed by Metro

Toronto officials) that the university was involved in secret negotiations with Metro Toronto to make a deal which would provide Metro with the land it needed south of Bloor for an intersection for the controversial Spadina Expressway and that part of the Huron-Sussex area might well be found to be needed not for university expansion but for a favor which the university was going to do the beleaguered builders of the expressway.

The Students' Administrative Council was less reticent about defending its activities regarding the Kensington land deal. Student politicians reassured each other that they had indeed stayed true to their principles of community participation in their actions in Kensington, and no doubt were grateful to provincial cabinet minister Allan Grossman who responded to public criticism of the province's role in this land deal by saying that the land could be in no more responsible hands than those of the Board of Education and by asking what could be a more worthy purpose for vacant land than putting up a new school.

Many people at the U of T wondered exactly what had happened in the Kensington land deal, but no one suggested the obvious: a public inquiry conducted by an impartial outsider, acceptable to all parties involved, and to whom people would agree to give sworn statements. Public inquiries are of course not an ideal means of discovering the truth, but in this situation an inquiry could probably have discovered what in fact went on and what the grounds were for the students' actions. Individuals at the university might have felt uneasy enough to have pressed for such an inquiry, but in fact no one did. The student politicians, just like the university administrators and the local cabinet minister, were able to make public statements about what "really" had happened with little fear that what they said would be subject to any closer scrutiny than that which a newspaper writer can provide.

Chapter Seven
City Politicians

Incredible. That has always been my reaction to city politicians ever since I encountered them for the first time two or three years ago. There is no other word for it: they are incredible.

This reaction is, of course, partly a product of the circumstances in which I have encountered city politicians. I met them first not because I went to law school with them, or because I found myself in the same back room at a political convention. Nor did I encounter my first city politician at a tea party, or on the phone when I asked for help in getting the sidewalk in front of my house fixed. If I had, no doubt my reactions would have been quite different. I would have regarded them as bad lawyers, or off-hand empty-headed women, or smooth operators in a world full of real estate agents and banana wholesalers. Instead I became acquainted with city politicians by watching them at work, in meetings at City Hall and with their constituents. All I know about most of them is how they operate in that situation. Most of them I have never spoken to, or seen on any other occasion. Most of them know me only because their desire for self-preservation dictated that they learn to detect me and my tape recorder at their meetings so that at the very least they would know when they risked having anything they said quoted to the world verbatim in an unsympathetic newspaper piece.

Of course it is a handicap not to know city politicians better, to be more knowledgeable about what sort of people they are, and what the interests are that lie behind their public actions. Yet the disadvantages are, for me, greatly outweighed by the advantage I have had of being able to write about the politicians as politicians, to comment on their public activities and their public style unhampered by the normal reticences of friends and acquaintances. To some extent I have been able to keep out of the city hall family world that encompasses politicians, officials, hangers-on, developers' lawyers, and city hall reporters. What I have written about the politicians at work has been the report of an outsider looking on.

What I have tried to do is to describe how the politicians act, how they conduct the affairs of city government. Instead of being obliged to report as succinctly as possible *what* they decided, *what* action they took, I have had the luxury (in the newspaper world, at least) of being able to take all that for granted, and to get down to describing *how* these decisions were arrived at and *how* they were justified in the public setting where they were taken.

I find as I read through these pieces on an average day at Toronto's Board of Control, the body which until 1970 functioned as the executive committee of the City Council, on an ordinary Board of Education meeting, and on a meeting where the Metropolitan Toronto Council chose its new chairman my reaction of incredulity is still there. I remain amazed that it is these people, operating this way, saying these things and using these reasons to explain themselves, who govern the city.

The four controllers on Toronto's Board of Control were elected in a city-wide vote until 1969 when the Board of Control was abolished in favor of an executive committee of aldermen elected by the aldermen themselves. The Board of Control had considerable power. This came partly from the fact that every resolution proposing expenditures had to pass through its hands before it got to City Council as a whole. The senior controller was responsible for preparation of the city's budget. To reverse a decision of the Board of Control required a two-thirds majority at City Council.

The politicians who were elected to the Board of Control were different from ward aldermen because they had to run in a city-wide election, and had to be known across the city. Once elected, they were obvious contenders for the post of mayor because they had a base of support in more than one ward. The normal course of events was that an alderman who was successful for one reason or another, who learned about city politics as an alderman and who was ambitious, ran for Board of Control. The one or two senior controllers, who after sitting on the Board of Control would be reasonably well-known political figures, would then run against an incumbent mayor (if they thought they had a chance) or would fight amongst themselves for the mayoralty when the incumbent retired.

The four members of the 1967-1969 Board of Control were Margaret Campbell, senior controller because she polled the most votes in the 1966 election, June Marks, Allan Lamport and Fred Beavis. Mr. Lamport was an old city politician who had been around for years and who had for a time been Toronto's mayor. Mrs. Marks had made a public reputation in the early 1960's as someone concerned about housing and the other problems of central-city residents, though she had been elected alderman only by winning the upper-middle-class Rosedale end of the Regent Park-Rosedale ward she had run in. Mr. Beavis was a long-time ward politician who had been elevated to the Board of Control from City Council in 1967 when the fourth controller elected in 1966, Herbert Orliffe, died. Presiding over the Board of Control was William Dennison, another long-time politician who had moved slowly through the ranks, from alderman to controller to senior controller. He had challenged the incumbent mayor, Philip Givens, in the 1966 election, along with another controller, William Archer, and in the three-way vote Mr. Dennison carried the working-class areas of the city and was elected.

October 27, 1969

An Ordinary Day at the Board of Control*

There is of course never a perfectly ordinary day at Toronto's Board of Control. Every Wednesday two or three different matters of some importance are discussed along with a long list of interchangeable subjects which have no general public interest.

What the Board of Control does on the matters both major and minor which come before it depends mainly on its two powerful members, Controller Margaret Campbell and Controller Allan Lamport. The crucial facet of Mrs. Campbell's political personality which is the basis of her power as a controller is her extensive and detailed knowledge of the city's business and her ability to grasp the significance of matters the board is discussing and to see their implications. It is not that Mrs. Campbell is capable of talking about any subject under the sun which happens to come up at the Board of Control; all the politicians can do that. What distinguishes her (and no doubt it will seem remarkable that this quality should mark her out from the others on the board) is that she is almost always sure about her facts and intelligent about the implications of the issue being discussed.

At the same time Mrs. Campbell is a very prudent politician. She is always aware of the interests of her colleagues and of the outsiders who are watching what she says and does, and she never casually acts in ways which disregard these interests.

*For another, not quite so ordinary, day in the life of this Board of Control see the National Film Board film *Flowers on a One-Way Street.*

Mrs. Campbell has always appeared more aware than most of the value of extending her base of personal political support across the city, and no doubt this has been one of the major factors behind her usual careful concern for the interests of all kinds of citizens' groups including both the most established (such as the Association of Women Electors) and the most recent (citizens' groups in downtown residential areas). Yet in spite of the differences between her political position and that of the old-guard majority at City Hall, Mrs. Campbell's interests are not all that much different on many matters from those of the other city politicians. This, combined with her obvious competence in the midst of so much incompetence, is what makes her a powerful person in Council and at the Board of Control.

The other powerful controller is Allan Lamport. Part of Mr. Lamport's strength comes from the fact that he is such a good blusterer — far too good to be ignored. More important at the Board of Control, however, is Mr. Lamport's position as one of three old ward politicians who share a single view about how city government should be run. For Mr. Lamport, Controller Fred Beavis, and Mayor William Dennison, city government is sewers and garbage collection for the people and high-rise development for the developers. The duty of the politicians to their constituents is to get action for someone whose street drain is blocked and to solve the problem of a pothole that hasn't been properly repaired. Apart from matters of this kind, the citizenry is expected to leave the business of governing in the hands of the politicians they elected.

At the Board of Control there is a certain amount of tension between Mrs. Campbell and Mr. Lamport, partly because they are different kinds of politicians. No doubt some of it also stems simply from the fact that each resents the other's power. The result is that the Lamport-Campbell tension is involved in almost everything that happens at every Board of Control meeting.

It was, for example, part of last Wednesday's ten-minute debate about whether Alderman Tony O'Donohue should be allowed to speak to the board. What exactly it was he wanted to talk about was never made clear. "Let's hear him," said Mrs. Campbell when the matter came up. The board agreed and Mr. O'Donohue began. He did not, however, address the controllers with the degree of humility usually expected from mere city aldermen. "I suppose I ought to be grateful for having this opportunity to speak on such an important item," he began. "If this isn't deputation day, I'm sure it's a courtesy . . ."

That's as far as he got. Mr. Lamport interrupted with an argument he apparently had only just thought of regarding why Mr. O'Donohue should not be allowed to speak at this meeting. The Mayor came briskly along bringing up the rear of Mr. Lamport's assault, saying that he hadn't had time to read the material on whatever it was Mr. O'Donohue wanted to talk about.

Mrs. Campbell tried to find out exactly what it was that Mr. O'Donohue proposed to discuss. Mr. O'Donohue began to tell her, but halfway into his first sentence he was interrupted by Mr. Lamport who reminded the Mayor petulantly that there was a motion on the floor to defer hearing Mr. O'Donohue for two weeks. The motion was put, and passed by the Lamport-Dennison-Beavis coalition.

Petty though this particular debate was, nevertheless it is discussions of this kind which take most of the time of the Board of Control's meetings. More important, this debate is a microcosm of the way in which the board makes all its decisions, including those on relatively important matters.

By far the most important issue which came up at last Wednesday's meeting was the proposed purchase by the city of a block of houses owned by one absentee owner in Trefann Court. This purchase marks the beginning of an attempt by City Council to implement an urban renewal plan in Trefann Court which will probably prove quite similar to the plan fought off by residents in 1966. The city's strategy is to implement its plan by purchasing properties on the open market for the time being while simultaneously claiming that there is as yet no plan for

Trefann. When and if one is drawn up, everyone at City Hall is saying residents will participate.

Trefann's residents' association realizes perfectly well that this strategy could succeed in ruling out any real influence by local people over the city's actions in Trefann. Mrs. Campbell has never given this association the same strong support she has given to other citizens' groups in other Toronto urban renewal areas. She was nevertheless the only person last Wednesday who gave any hint of understanding and worrying about the real significance of the proposal to buy this block of properties.

The questions she asked about it were sufficiently complicated that none of the down-the-line supporters of the proposal on the Board of Control could have answered them. Development Commissioner Graham Emslie leaped into the gap with a long string of reassurances. He made his strategy of implementing a plan while pretending that it doesn't exist into a positive virtue: "I have never agreed," he said, "to the old and extremely arbitrary and artificial distinction between the planning stages and implementation stages in urban renewal."

Nor, said Mr. Emslie in noting this particular personal conviction of his, do many of the members of the Board of Control believe in making this distinction. This was his pointed reminder to Mrs. Campbell that he had already succeeded in lining up the Board of Control majority to support his strategy to get around Trefann's residents and to get the city's hands on provincial and federal money to pay another few months' salary for Mr. Emslie and his department.

As soon as Mr. Emslie had recorded his rationalization of the proposal, Mr. Lamport moved quickly to cut off further debate or comment from Mrs. Campbell. The mayor lost no time in agreeing with Mr. Lamport's objection that discussing the plan for Trefann was out of order. His comment on the proposed purchase indicates the sophistication of his understanding of the issue the board was in the midst of deciding. "The thing that is before us is shall we buy the houses," said the mayor. "Do we think that they're a good bargain? "

Mr. Beavis lined himself up with Mr. Dennison and Mr. Lamport. His comment suggested that he too understood only the simplest aspect of the decision the board was making. "For God's sake," he said, "let's get on with Trefann. We've been talking about it for three or four years, battering it back and forth, and, well, this is one of the most important matters, is to get these houses down so we can do a little bit of resting at night so that we don't have a major fire in the area which has always worried me . . ."

Where does June Marks stand in all this? In the eyes of the other politicians, Mrs. Marks is an entertainment. She is rarely if ever taken seriously. Given the situation on the Board of Control, however, it usually doesn't matter what she does. If there is a split, she can side with Mrs. Campbell and Mrs. Campbell loses 3-2; if Mrs. Marks sides with the others, Mrs. Campbell loses 4-1. There appears to be no consistent pattern in what Mrs. Marks does. The Trefann discussion is a good illustration of this. Of course Mrs. Marks made her city-wide reputation as a crusader against slum landlords and bad housing conditions. Last Wednesday, however, she explained her support for the city buying the proposed block of properties in Trefann in terms not of what it did for tenants or area residents but of how good it was for their owner. "I'm pleased," said Mrs. Marks, "I'm pleased for the landlords because I think there's been nothing but strife here; I know I've caused a lot of it . . . All these homes had to have their hydro updated two or three years ago, and the owner only put the rent up $5 at that particular time."

Both Mrs. Marks and Mrs. Campbell ended by voting in favor of the city's purchase. But before they did so they raised some important questions about exactly what the city is now doing in Trefann Court, questions which reflected some concern about the interests of local people in the matter. Mr. Lamport, Mr. Beavis and Mr. Dennison had no questions at all.

In the debate last Wednesday and in the normal way

the Board of Control operates is to be found the explanation of Mr. Dennison's role as mayor, and of the support he has been receiving from many people on City Council. Mr. Dennison proves to be just one more member of the old-guard majority at City Hall. Because he is not a strong person and because he is almost never on top of any of the issues the city is dealing with, he does not function as a leader of the old-guard group. Even as chairman of Board of Control and City Council, he rarely takes procedural initiatives but instead relies (as he did when Mr. O'Donohue wanted to speak to the board) on his political associates for constant guidance.

The bulk of the board's time last week as every week was spent not in discussing the important issues raised by the proposed purchase of properties in Trefann. Instead it was spent contemplating the Milk Act, preparing strategy for some haggling with a developer about how he should pay for some city land he is buying, listening to aldermen on their pet peeves (like Alice Summerville who last Wednesday proposed that all glass bottles be abolished in the city of Toronto), and fighting about whether they should listen to Tony O'Donohue for five minutes. Perhaps it is not so surprising that in this kind of world it is Allan Lamport, Fred Beavis, and William Dennison who survive and prosper.

* * *

Toronto's Board of Education is a practice field for budding city politicians. The result is that most of its members fall into one of two categories — long-time trustees who were not good enough politicians to make the jump from the board to City Council, and young politicians readying themselves for a promotion. A third and much less important category of trustees is people who have been teachers or who have worked in education in some way and who, when they retire, decide to become part-time amateur politicians to keep themselves busy.

November 17, 1969

**Breaking up the home
at the Board of Education**

Toronto's Board of Education does not have much important business to discuss. The kind of decisions the board is usually to be found making was well-illustrated by its debate last Thursday night over whether a meeting scheduled for this Tuesday with parents' organizations should be held at 4:30 or 5:30 and by the discussion about whether one of the board's psychiatrists should be allowed to lecture two hours a week at the University of Toronto.

Board members seem to be most at home when they are contemplating (as happened in a property committee meeting I was at last spring) two different kinds of steel lockers solemnly set out for their inspection or arguing furiously about how high an upright piano can be and still allow the average teacher to see over its top.

Much of the little important business it does the board conducts in secret. All discussions and decisions about school sites and expropriation, for instance, are closed to the public.

Given the subjects which they spend most of their time talking about, it should not be surprising that the trustees have developed childish and petty ways of going about their business, unconsciously imitating some of the silliest rituals of the educational system they are supposed to be managing. Thus, for instance, like so many children in Grade Three, they answer "present" when their names are called in a little roll-call which starts each meeting. The board has a rule that trustees and people in the gallery cannot smoke when the board is in session, but can smoke when the board is meeting in committee of the whole.

Concentrating as much as they do on what are really non-issues, questions of small administrative detail, members appear to have developed a means of avoiding the few real issues which do come before them. This they do sometimes by trivializing what are important matters, sometimes by refusing to understand what is said to them, sometimes by ordinary straight-forward evasion.

At last Thursday's meeting — with municipal elections only two weeks away and with a gallery of about 75 people interested in what the board would do with one of the items on its agenda — one might have expected that at least some trustees would break away from their usual form to make a strong impression on this audience and in the press. But it was business absolutely as usual for all the trustees except Alan Archer. Mr. Archer, who appears to be having some trouble in his ward over the board's decision to expropriate 51 houses on Cornwall and Oak Streets, was uncharacteristically silent at this meeting.

Most of the people present were there to see what the board would do about an after-school program to be run in a number of schools across the city. But there were three people who attended to put what proved to be a second real issue before the meeting: a proposal that special school assemblies be organized by principals, teachers and students in high schools to discuss the war in Vietnam.

Board chairman Alex Thompson said he felt this proposal was not "within our purview," but a mild objection from one trustee quickly persuaded him to change his mind. Trustee Mahlon Beach seconded the motion that the spokesman for the Vietnam Mobilization Committee and Students Against the War in Vietnam be heard. "If we don't give them a chance to be heard," said Mr. Beach, "we're giving them the opportunity to say that we are trying to muzzle expression of thought. There's just one question I would like to ask," he went on. "Is this a Communist-front organization? "

The group's spokesman, Joe Young, ignored Mr. Beach's question and started to address the board. Instead of thanking the board for its great kindness in hearing him, however, he said that he was glad that the board chairman had reconsidered his opinion that the matter was not relevant to the board's business.

Trustee William Lang objected immediately: "I'm very happy to listen to this gentleman's views, but I don't think he should stand here and criticize the chairman of this board or the members of this board. We'd like to hear his opinion on the subject, but I don't think he has any right to stand here and criticize this board . . ."

When Mr. Young said that he felt he had been perfectly in order in what he had said, Trustee Irene McBrien interrupted again: "I think Mr. Chairman, if this continues, that I would move that we do not hear this speaker. He has shown no courtesy or common decency . . ."

Mr. Young went on and made his proposal that the board permit and encourage school assemblies. When he finished, the chairman asked if there were any questions and Mr. Beach was on his feet:

"I have a number of questions, Mr. Chairman. First one: Is this a Communist-front organization? "

Mr. Young gave an answer which amounted to saying that it was not.

"Were you born in Canada, Mr. Young? " asked Mr. Beach.

"That's an irrelevant question."

"Then," said Mr. Beach, "I assume you were not born in Canada . . . You are too young to be a war veteran. Are you married? "

Mr. Beach did not ask Mr. Young whether he was now or ever had been a member of the Communist Party; instead he went on to misinterpret Mr. Young's request.

Trustee Ernest Jones did much the same thing. He seemed to interpret the proposal as a suggestion that the board participate in the Vietnam war. "Mr. Chairman," said Mr. Jones, "I'm very much surprised at my colleagues at allowing this stuff to be spoken here tonight. There are many veterans here who served in the Second World War. Why did they fight? They fought for democracy. They fought to give these people better rights, a better say in this country. And, furthermore, I think it's out of the jurisdiction of this board to interfere with Vietnam at all. I think it's not our duty."

Trustees Barry Lowes, Ying Hope, Maurice Lister and

William Ross then got involved in the discussion. Mr. Ross chided Mr. Beach very gently for his leading and irrelevant questions and complained about how Mr. Jones always brought up the matter of who had and who had not fought in the Second World War. But none of these trustees went so far as to state clearly a position on Mr. Young's request; rather they slid out from under the matter by saying that matters like this were the responsibility not of the board but of school principals.

Of course this request, made the day before the November 1969 Vietnam mobilization march in the United States, was formulated at least partly with the expectation that it would produce this kind of response from board members. Nevertheless, it did raise a real and important issue: the question of how the schools deal with subjects like Vietnam on which teachers, students and board members have strongly-held divergent views. Not only did the trustees avoid talking about how the schools should deal with such subjects; they managed to escape obtaining any more than the barest possible minimum amount of information about how topics of this kind are in fact being tackled at present.

The second major issue dealt with at last Thursday's meeting was the proposal of the Social Planning Council's Toronto Area Council for a demonstration project for after-school programs in three different kinds of schools across the city. Mrs. Judy Jordan read a brief describing the proposal. The program would be financed by the board, would take place in school buildings and would be staffed by paid workers. Control of the program would, according to Mrs. Jordan, be partly in the hands of what the brief called "indigenous people," a revealingly awkward term for parents and residents of the area served by the school where the program was being run.

One board committee which had discussed this proposal gave it enthusiastic endorsement. A second refused to propose funds to run it in more than one school. With the public galleries full of people interested in seeing what the board would do on this matter, the trustees were conscious that they could easily find themselves in trouble if they did not satisfy the project's supporters.

Trustee William Ross was on his feet as soon as Mrs. Jordan had read her brief. He wanted to know how she would react to a proposal that the whole matter be referred to a special committee of the board which would meet with people from the Social Planning Council. This committee would get down to work immediately and it could — not would — report back to the board in time for its November 27 meeting, the last one scheduled before the December 1 elections. To Mr. Ross's immense relief, Mrs. Jordan did not object. Mr. Ross then gave people in the audience the impression that this move would save the $25,000 proposed for this program by the board's finance committee in the board's 1970 budget.

"What I would want, Mr. Chairman," said Mr. Ross, "is that the sum of $25,000 be included in the 1970 budget . . . What I would like to do is secure a sum of money . . . and then, set up a subcommittee . . . to work out this program so we can come in with the project." Yet the effect of Mr. Ross's motion was to allow the board to avoid approving any money for the program. But that was not the impression Mr. Ross gave Mrs. Jordan and her supporters and they raised no objection to his proposal. The result was that all the trustees, those in favor and those opposed, could vote for Mr. Ross's motion.

The issue was successfully avoided, which is just as well considering how harmful it might have been in the election campaign. Nevertheless, many trustees trotted out their arguments concerning this proposal and showed how they were prepared to trivialize and misunderstand it.

Trustee Irene McBrien said that the trouble with the program was that children would be staying at school until 6 or 6:30 and then would have to go home when it was dark. "It would be very dark and dangerous for children going home by themselves," she said. That was not the only consideration Mrs. McBrien had in mind. "Now if a child is going to be in school from 9 to 6:30 or 7," she said, "I think they're going to get tired of school altogether."

Trustee Ernest Lang had a different reason for being unhappy about the proposal. "This board will be dissolving itself very shortly ... We can't at the last meeting of this board commit a newly elected board."

Mahlon Beach had two objections. "I don't think this comes under the jurisdiction of the Board of Education," he said, "I think it's Parks and Recreation." His second reason: "The increasing number of mothers who go to work is causing increased crime. The prevalence of working mothers is increasing ... I'm wondering if we are supporting a program like this, and I feel that there is a need for a program, are we encouraging mothers to work; are we encouraging the breaking up of the home, of the family?"

Trustee Kenneth Carson had a final addition to the set of reasons being assembled to explain a vote which, fortunately, the trustees were now going to be able to avoid. "There is a need here," he said, "but I'm afraid that it's going to be abused. I'm afraid we're going to increase our costs and we're getting through to people who do not need the service but they're going to use it because it's there, because it's being offered by this board ... I hope we're not enticing mothers to go to work as a result of us having this extra baby-sitting session."

Just like the proposal for school assemblies on Vietnam, the proposed after-school program is an important suggestion and it raises a number of issues: what control parents should have over school activities, for example, and how desirable it is to have schools become even more dominant in children's lives. These issues were all avoided, partly by Mr. Ross's evasions, partly by other trustees' incomprehension and trivializing.

And so, in its own amazing, unbelievable way, the board found itself at the end of another meeting in which it carried out its responsibility for running the city's school system. Mr. Beach had an opportunity to ask an anti-Vietnam war student if his group was a Communist front; Mr. Jones had a chance to talk about fighting for democracy in the Second World War; Mr. Carson analyzed an after-school program as an enticement to women to go out to work. Those of us in the public gallery observed all this and felt a curious combination of rage, despair, amusement and astonishment.

* * *

There are two levels of municipal government in Toronto. The Metropolitan Toronto Council is responsible for major roads, sewer and water systems (though not local ones), administration of general welfare and family assistance programs, large-scale city planning (though not detailed matters like urban renewal or zoning), large-scale parks and recreation facilities, and a number of less important matters. The Metro Council has 32 members, all of whom are politicians elected to the councils of the City of Toronto or of the five boroughs which together comprise "Metro." Toronto's 12 members on the Metro Council are (as of 1970) the mayor and the alderman from each of the city's 11 wards who received the most votes in the previous election.

The Metro Toronto Council has a chairman whose job has in practice had much more power and authority attached to it than have the jobs of the mayors of Toronto and the five boroughs.* The first chairman, Frederick Gardiner, was appointed by the provincial government which also decided the form that metropolitan government would take in Toronto. Subsequent chairmen, the provincial legislation laid down, were to be elected by the Metro Council.

When the second Metro chairman, William Allen, decided to retire in 1969, an election by Metro Council members was held to choose his successor. At the election meeting, the four candidates for the post made speeches, and voting took place immediately after. All four candi-

---

*On the structure of metropolitan government in Toronto, see Harold Kaplan, *Urban Political Systems*. New York: Columbia University Press, 1967.

dates were experienced politicians. Three, Jack MacBeth, Norman Goodhead, and Albert Campbell, were from the suburban boroughs. David Rotenberg, the fourth candidate, was the only city politician who ran. Mr. Rotenberg came last in the voting; Albert Campbell, at the time mayor of the borough of Scarborough, was elected. I wrote an article about the election speeches which preceded the voting.

October 6, 1969

"There Aren't Many Churchills"

"Now there aren't many Churchills or Lincolns or Fred Gardiners." That is a sentence to be treasured, ten words which sum up the remarkable world of Metropolitan Toronto politicians, the world of the people who, with little outside interference, selected last Tuesday the man who is really the mayor (although he is not called the mayor) of Metro Toronto. Fittingly, the man who spoke this line, former Scarborough reeve Ab Campbell, will himself probably be enshrined in several years in the Toronto political pantheon. It will be the names Churchill, Lincoln, Gardiner and Ab Campbell that a speaker ten years from now will be proudly listing at a similar meeting of similar (if not the same) people.

Of course it is true that last Tuesday's meeting was only a formal run-through in public of what had already been decided in private. Metro's 32 electors did not decide how they would vote at this public session where, for the one and only time, all 32 electors saw all four candidates lined up in front of them, one after the other explaining for the record exactly who they were and what they stood for. The election was settled, as the newspapers have recorded, in Alderman Oscar Sigsworth's living room, in a hospitality suite at the Inn on the Park, and perhaps in the private lounge at the back of the council chamber at City Hall.

Yet, even though last Tuesday's meeting was only a

formality, there was a certain sense of occasion and of importance about it. This was most apparent in the public gallery. The gallery was jammed, but it was not the ordinary citizens of Metro who were there to watch Metro's mayor being elected. Almost everyone present was a somebody in the Metro political world. Of course, former mayor Phil Givens was there, and school trustee William Ross, the city's chief planner Dennis Barker and June Rowlands of the Association of Women Electors. Almost all of the city politicians who do not sit on Metro Council were there, too.

These people were, however, intermingled with another important group in Metro politics, the developers and their smooth, expensive lawyers who are often to be seen at City Hall unveiling yet another major development proposal or requesting some slight variation in the official plan or in the city's bylaws to allow a particular project to proceed. Interestingly, there were not several sub-groups of somebodies, the developers over here, lawyers over there, politicians all in a row, newspaper people in a special corner. Everyone appeared to be part of the same large group. The row of people at the front of the section where I was sitting was typical. From left to right were Alderman Helen Johnston, Alderman Harold Menzies, former city development commissioner Walter Manthorpe, principal owner of Meridian Property Management Ltd. Phil Roth, Alderman Ben Grys, a blonde woman I didn't recognize, and Alderman Joe Piccininni. The decision these people had come to see made had already been settled, but their presence was certainly testimony to the importance this choice has in their world.

What happened last Tuesday was that for more than an hour there were speeches on behalf of each candidate by the nominator, the seconder, and then the candidate himself. Immediately after the speeches, the voting took place and everything was settled in 20 minutes. It was, of course, the voting which attracted all the attention. The speeches were nothing but a sort of liturgical bow in the direction of democratic formalities. Yet they deserve to be noticed because of what they said about the articles

Curiously, though there were four candidates, there was only one speech made. Each of the four gave a slightly different version of this one speech; all that changed was the order in which the obligatory things were said. Only David Rotenberg's speech was significantly different, and the way in which it was different at least partly explains why he ran last in the election.

The first thing three of the candidates said was something about their humbleness and a sense of their own imperfections. One of the reasons for putting this at the beginning was to get it as far away as possible from the ringing declarations of superior qualities with which each candidate closed his speech.

Ab Campbell: "First of all I want to say to Mayor Davidson and Mayor Service . . . moving my motion [nomination] and seconding my motion there: I wasn't quite sure you were talking about me."

Jack MacBeth, speaking about his nominator, Alderman Mary Temple: "I am particularly indebted to Mrs. Temple, because it's a mystery to me why such a well-known lady of good reputation and a tender heart has lent her name to such a scoundrel."

Mr. Rotenberg, referring to the speech by his nominator, Controller June Marks: "Having listened to Controller Marks' speech, I hesitated even to address you. She said it all so beautifully."

Only Norman Goodhead omitted a few opening humble remarks, and neglected even to imply any personal shortcomings.

The next important point in The Candidate's Speech was to assess Toronto as a city, the Metro government system, and the history of Metro and its two previous chairman. Only Mr. Campbell linked Churchill and Lincoln with the first Metro chairman, Fred Gardiner. He forgot to say what a great city Toronto is, but he did describe the post of Metro chairman as "one of the most important positions in Metropolitan Toronto, yes, in the province of Ontario, or in all of Canada." Mr. Goodhead, in a voice which completely overwhelmed his physical presence and which I can describe only as a Crang Plaza voice (like the radio advertisements for Crang Plaza Motors), rushed headlong into total extravagance about Toronto and its Metro government: "I can tell you right here and right now that we have the finest form of metropolitan government, of regional government there is in the world today."

Mr. Goodhead paid his respects to past Metro chairmen: "I hardly need to tell this gathering how much, much credit for the growth that we know is directly contributed to Frederick G. 'Big Daddy' Gardiner, and I don't think he's here today and I just wish he were, and to Bill Allen — and let me tell you that there aren't very many Bill Allens left in this world and let's hope that we can find one here today who will carry on in the same tradition that Bill has carried on."

Mr. MacBeth broke with The Speech to the extent of saying that Metro does have its faults and its problems. These lasted through only three sentences. Then he was back on the track with references to Gardiner and Allen, and: "This council has achieved an enviable record, each council building on the record of previous councils, building, enlarging and improving . . . until today this municipality is one recognized throughout the world as a leader and a good place to live."

Only Mr. Rotenberg abandoned The Speech at this point to talk about Metro government in terms recognizable to ordinary citizens who are not Metro politicians and who follow city politics in the newspapers. His assessment of Metro sounded almost like a criticism: "If our community . . . is to achieve the goals of human fulfilment which we all hold, Metro must fill its role as the co-ordinator of local municipal governments, not as a competitor."

The third important point in The Speech was to stress the candidate's clear awareness of the need for everyone — not everyone in the city, but every one of the politicians of Metro Toronto — to recognize their common interest in working together and in identifying themselves with the

"Metro family." The term was Mr. Campbell's: "I feel it very necessary to bring about more harmony in the family of Metro Toronto politicians and I will make that on the list of high priorities, on the list of duties that I would have to perform."

Mr. Goodhead said virtually the same thing, only more aggressively: "There must be an awareness and a recognition that the future of Metro is critically dependent on the way in which we, and I say we, ladies and gentlemen, together resolve the problems of today." When he said this, Mr. Goodhead was looking at the 32 ladies and gentlemen who were just about to vote in the election, not at the 300 or 400 ladies and gentlemen in the gallery or at the public beyond.

Mr. MacBeth: "I say that it is enthusiasm and confidence that this council needs. And I am sure that this is the spirit and the timbre it will have in the years ahead."

Mr. Rotenberg said much the same thing, though the real world was not quite so far away from his version: "In choosing a chairman to lead this council in the months, perhaps in the years, ahead we are filling a post in which the occupant must be able to work with the members of the Metropolitan Corporation not as a rival for power but as a partner for progress."

The Speech then required each candidate to enumerate his own qualities and abilities. Mr. Campbell and Mr. Goodhead did this directly. Mr. MacBeth and Mr. Rotenberg were a bit less brash, but no more modest.

This led to the final pitch, for everyone except Mr. Rotenberg who managed to sandwich the obligatory material into the first few paragraphs and the last bit of his speech, leaving a good chunk of time free to sketch his view of the functions of Metro government and of the role of the chairman. He talked about the participation of citizens in the widest possible range of Metro government activities, certainly not the most discreet subject to bring up before the 32 people about to be the only voters in the election for the real mayor of a city of two million.

The last few lines of The Speech were humble and

assertive at the same time, the exact combination depending on the candidate. "I offer to this council and to the citizens of Metropolitan Toronto," said Mr. Campbell, "a lifetime of experience in the municipal field, a dedication to the work, and that I will be fair and give equal consideration to all alike, and that I have a great desire to serve the metropolitan area which I love very much."

"I tell you, ladies and gentlemen," said Mr. Goodhead, "today I offer myself to you to carry on these responsibilities if it is in your wisdom that I be the ·chairman of the Metropolitan Corporation for the period and the balance of nineteen hundred and sixty-nine."

"Ladies and gentlemen," said Mr. MacBeth, his voice dropping almost to a confidential whisper, "I ask your support for that leadership."

Mr. Rotenberg, by this time almost back on the track after his digression into the real world and his excursion into policy matters: "The citizens of Metropolitan Toronto are not interested in commitments or deals or favors or friendships. They are trusting to us to choose the man who will be best for the entire community. I am prepared for this job. I ask for your support."

Of the four candidates, of course, it was Mr. Rotenberg who was furthest away from getting the support he requested. He was also furthest away from the comfortable, self-centred, self-satisfied world of which he is nevertheless part, and to which the other three candidates were uniformly and totally committed. It is a world in which the politicians are one big family, where virtually all the important people can take the afternoon off (or get paid for going) and fit into the City Council chamber to watch one of their number selected for the office of the city's super-mayor, where Metropolitan government is wonderful, Toronto itself is wonderful, and Frederick Gardiner is a Lincoln or a Churchill or both. Of course, no one really believes it, but what a strange fantasy world for three or four otherwise quite different men to share even for one afternoon of public speaking and job hunting.

* * *

Along with the meetings of the bodies to which they are elected, city politicians appear at another kind of public meeting where they are required to discuss political issues and to explain and defend their views and their actions. Normally this happens at meetings of citizens' groups, residents' associations and businessmen's associations. During election campaigns, activities of this kind are stepped up and candidates appear at countless public meetings where they are questioned by their constituents.

It is not often at public meetings of this kind that city politicians can get away with making speeches which say nothing or with expressing platitudinous, empty views on world affairs. Their audiences usually include some people who know the issues, know the politicians' records, and want to pin them down on what they have done. Recording exactly what is said at these meetings always makes politicians very unhappy. It also fills in another dimension of the incredible world of city politics.

I wrote about the all-candidates' meeting held by Don Vale's Homeowners' and Residents' Association for the eight candidates who were running in the December 1969 election in the new Ward Seven. One of the candidates in the election was John Sewell, a lawyer who had been working for the previous three years as a community organizer in Trefann Court and then in other parts of the ward, including Cornwall-Oak, south of St. James Town and Berkeley and Wilkins. Sewell ran as an independent. Another strong candidate was Karl Jaffary, also a lawyer who had lived in Don Vale since 1966 and who had been president of the Don Vale residents' association during its first year. Jaffary, long active in the New Democratic Party and a member of the party's national council, was running as the NDP's only candidate in the ward.

The other candidate who was an obviously-serious contender in the election was Oscar Sigsworth, a long-term ward politician from the old Ward One which lay east of the Don River. Sigsworth was running in a ward which was one-third his former ward, two-thirds unknown to him. His record and his performance at City Hall left no doubt that he was one of the group of eight or ten aldermen who strongly supported the interests of developers at City Hall. Indeed, as Sigsworth stated at the Don Vale meeting, his links to the construction-development world were extremely close.

Much to everyone's surprise, Sigsworth showed up at the all-candidates meeting in Don Vale. His performance, especially the views he expressed about his job at City Hall and his responsibilities to listen to his constituents, were a very good illustration of the views of the majority group of politicians who like nothing better than constituents who take no interest whatsoever in what their politicians are doing, and who come out to vote for the alderman who got the storm sewer unplugged in front of their house four years ago.

November 24, 1969

"I Won't Be a Charlie McCarthy"*

Last Monday's election meeting organized by the Don Vale Association of Homeowners and Residents was for all the aldermanic candidates running in the new Ward Seven but it turned out to be Oscar Sigsworth Night. It was the first time Don Vale residents have encountered Mr. Sigsworth, at present alderman for Ward One, which lies east of the Don River.

What made last Monday's meeting a special occasion was that it illustrated very well what an "old guard" city politician is, and what happens when such politicians and people active in citizens' groups and concerned about city

---

*This article was not published by the *Globe and Mail*. It would have appeared exactly a week before the 1969 municipal elections, and the *Globe's* editors felt that it was not a fair comment on the Ward Seven campaign because I was at the time working for John Sewell, one of the aldermanic candidates in the ward. This was the only time during the six-months' series that the *Globe* raised an objection to what I had written and refused to print my article as it was written. On two other occasions there were objections raised because of possible libel problems, but these were ironed out and the articles were published in a form which was perfectly satisfactory to me.

politics confront each other.

"Old guard" is, of course, a phrase that flits through election speeches and newspaper columns with no one being too precise about exactly what it means and whom it refers to. One thing it means, everyone is agreed, is a consistent willingness to support developers over the objections of local residents on controversial rezoning and redevelopment proposals. On the nine votes on eight controversial rezoning and development issues of this kind which have been tabulated by the Confederation of Residents and Ratepayers Associations (CORRA), Mr. Sigsworth has the best record of all from the point of view of developers, the worst from the point of view of citizens' groups. He ties with Controller Fred Beavis, with eight votes against ratepayers' associations, none in favor. There is no doubt that Mr. Sigsworth belongs in the "old guard" category.

None of the other candidates running in Ward Seven have been on City Council, so none can properly be called "old guard." There are two types of aldermanic hopefuls in the ward. The first is candidates who have been active in the ward's political problems of the last few years. John Sewell, running as an independent, has worked full-time in the ward for three years for the Trefann Court Residents' Association and for a number of other citizens' groups. Karl Jaffary, running on the NDP ticket, was president of the Don Vale residents' association in 1967-68 when the organization was beating off the city's first plan for the area, which involved substantial expropriation. He is now on that association's executive.

The other group of candidates are newcomers, people who have had little or no involvement in dealing with urban renewal, expropriation, and redevelopment. These include Mike Doran, an independent, Doug Loney, running for the Liberals, and Charlie Rolfe, also an independent. Sam Rotenberg, operator of a variety store on Parliament Street, is active in the Ward Two Businessmen's Association but has not had any direct contact with urban renewal planning.

Last Monday's meeting come to life only when Mr. Sigsworth arrived a few minutes late. It didn't take him long to get to his explanation of why he is running in the new Ward Seven.

He noted that the block ward boundaries split the old Ward One where he and Controller Fred Beavis were elected in 1966. "I had to make a decision whether I would take one half of Ward One or the other, in view of the fact that the ward was split. The people there have been very good to me," Mr. Sigsworth said, "so I decided that I would make a choice, along with Controller Fred Beavis who is my running mate and alderman. And we decided that we would each take half of the ward, for better or for worse. I took this half, Fred Beavis took the other, and we're going to see how it turns out."

I took this half, Fred Beavis took the other: Mr. Sigsworth made it quite clear that he considered Don Vale as territory to be divided up amongst the sitting aldermen at City Hall.

Candidates were asked about election expenses and sources of campaign funds. The budgets quoted by the other candidates ranged from $500 to $3000, though Mr. Rotenberg refused to estimate his expenses. All said they were relying on small contributions, with no money coming from developers, except for Mr. Rotenberg who said he has received $110 in contributions and that his wife is paying the rest of his expenses.

Mr. Sigsworth also detailed his financial situation. "I've received $5000," he said, " and I expect to contribute $2000 myself. A great deal of my money has come from people in the contracting business because I am associated with the contracting field. And it is my conviction that they believe in good government and they are willing to contribute to it, just as they are willing to contribute to the United Appeal."

A great deal of my money has come from people in the contracting business: Mr. Sigsworth was making no bones about the fact that his money was coming mostly from contractors and developers, and he made a point of saying that he has personal connections to this field. In fact he works in public relations for a large ready-mix concrete firm.

Just to remove any possible source of confusion, the close similarity between contractors and developers was pointed out to Mr. Sigsworth. His amiable reply: "I wouldn't be surprised if one or two developers contributed to my campaign, right."

People at the meeting then zeroed in on Mr. Sigsworth's voting record at City Hall, and noted his score on the CORRA tabulations — eight votes for developers, none for their ratepayer oppostion.

"I suggest to you," said Mr. Sigsworth, "that the people who were opposed to those applications were a small percentage, even a fractional percentage of the citizens of Toronto."

"But these people," protested his questioner, "were representing the people in their areas."

"I think you elect people to make decisions," replied Mr. Sigsworth. "I don't think you elect people to be Charlie McCarthys for the public afterwards."

Charlie McCarthys for the public? That is evidently what Mr. Sigsworth calls aldermen who pay serious attention to the views of ratepayers', and citizens' groups on City Council.

Another questioner went after Mr. Sigsworth on his record on the Don Mount urban renewal scheme which is located in his old ward. Mr. Sigsworth was asked what he had done when Don Mount holdout Mrs. Dorothy Graham refused to move on the grounds that her expropriation compensation offer from the city was much less than a "home for a home."

Mr. Sigsworth responded by listing some of the good works which he has achieved for the people of Ward One.

"I just happen to have built a $7 million public housing project at Blake Street, I just happen to be responsible for a $1.5 million senior citizens' home on Logan. If that isn't being concerned with the people, I don't know what is."

I just happen to have built? The Blake Street project is an OHC development; the senior citizens' housing on Logan was put up by WoodGreen Community Centre.

Mr. Sigsworth was not the only candidate at last Monday's meeting who was questioned by Don Vale residents. The other candidates were also asked their views on the Don Vale plan, on decision-making power for citizens and citizens' groups, on the airport, on amalgamation, and on party politics.

Mr. Doran arrived too late to answer more than one or two questions. Mr. Rolfe generally limited himself to agreeing with what someone else said. Mr. Loney, the Liberal candidate, expressed his good intentions and concern for the people of the ward. Mr. Rotenberg went off on a number of sidetracks.

Mr. Jaffary criticized the kind of aldermen Don Vale has had in the past: "The people we've been voting for in the past have been utterly unresponsive to anything we wanted." He proposed a ward citizens' council, hedged a bit when asked if he would always take his instructions from this council, but stated firmly: "Any time that a representative body of people come from this ward and say 'This is what we want' then that's what I'm doing."

Mr. Sewell said that he felt aldermen should be directly involved in helping to start and working with citizens' groups. "This is probably the most effective way of finding out what that community happens to want," he said. "My function as an alderman would be to make sure that the people of this community got together and expressed their opinions, and told me what to say as alderman, so that I would be a mouthpiece for them."

The last question asked at the meeting was directed to Mr. Sigsworth, and was concerned with how much attention he was prepared to give the views of organized groups of people in his ward.

"If you're asking," replied Mr. Sigsworth, "am I receptive to people, the answer's yes. Yes. I listen to people, for sure."

It was a fitting end for Oscar Sigsworth Night in Don Vale.

* * *

Conclusion

In the Board of Education's actions regarding the Cornwall-Oak school site, in the activities of city officials and politicians regarding urban renewal, in the treatment accorded Berkeley-Wilkins tenants by OHC, in the experiences of Trefann Court children and mothers with the school system, the politicians and officials who operate these public bureaucracies were acting in their normal, usual manner. What is different about these issues is that the pople involved organized themselves to get hold of and use political power in order to influence the conduct of the government body they were dealing with, and at the very least to try to ensure that they were not harmed directly by government decisions and policies.

In all the cases discussed here, political organizations came about because people found themselves faced with an immediate and serious threat; organizing themselves into a group was a last-ditch effort at self-protection. Urban renewal expropriation produced residents' organizations in Don Vale, Trefann and Kensington; the University of Toronto's expansion plans produced the Huron-Sussex Residents' Association; town house renovators and OHC produced the Wilkins-Berkeley tenants' group; the Board of Education created the Cornwall-Oak residents' organization.

The reaction of politicians and officials to those citizen organizations has been the same: while saying how wonderful it is to have citizens interested in politics and in government, the politicians and officials have done their best to discourage people from organizing and to weaken and destroy groups that manage to establish themselves. In the Cornwall-Oak area, ward school trustee Alan Archer counselled residents not to bother trying to do anything about the Board of Education's expropriation because there was nothing they could do to stop it. In Don Vale city officials and politicians pretended that one residents' group, the Don Vale Property Owners' Association, which made no pretence of having members, open meetings, or elections was to be taken as seriously as another group which paid careful attention to these matters, but which was not so friendly to the city in its policy views. OHC quietly advised Wilkins-Berkeley tenants to forget their ideas of dealing with OHC as a group via a lawyer if they really wanted to get into public housing. For politicians and bureaucrats, citizen participation ceases being wonderful the moment it begins to happen to them.

Though the chapters in this book record the experiences of different groups of people, faced with widely differing problems, dealing with a wide range of public bodies and agencies, there is a remarkable consistency in their experiences with government in its various forms. Lies, deception, and incredible errors came naturally to both politicians and officials when these served their purposes; keeping essential information secret was a matter of course. Thus Trustee Alan Archer talked grandly about vacant land worth perhaps $30 a square foot at a time when it was clear that a reasonable estimate would have been $10. The Board of Education said it was "reconsidering" a decision when it was busy carrying it so far that it would be impossible to reverse. The University of Toronto's Students' Administrative Council said it was anxious to cooperate with local people and was prepared to give them a veto over any development proposal while it worked up in secret first one scheme and then a second which were both to be implemented with little regard for local views.

A second experience common to these citizens in their encounters with city government was the unwillingness of public bodies to respect people's most basic rights, their right to fair treatment and their right to be protected from unnecessary and arbitrary direct harm as a result of public actions and public policies. Fairness and equity played no part whatsoever in the discussion of Board of Education trustees on the issue of compensation for tenants in the Cornwall-Oak area. OHC made a great show of its point-system priority lists for public housing applicants, but kept point scores and priorities secret and made it impossible for anyone to determine whether these were fairly arrived at and respected in the corporation's decision-making.

Depressing though these generalizations may be, there is one more common element in the experiences of the citizens of Toronto which are recorded here which is even more depressing. It is that, in spite of all their efforts, in spite of the clear justice of their case, in spite of their success at making their issue a public matter, they got nowhere. The Cornwall-Oak demolition went ahead. Tenants were offered no compensation. Opportunity classes in downtown schools went on as usual. Planning for Trefann Court got underway on the city's terms. OHC's admissions system was unchanged, and applicants were subsequently not allowed to negotiate with OHC as groups. The U of T continued buying up and demolishing houses.

Only in the ward boundaries dispute did citizens make clear progress, and this result stemmed from the fact that the crucial decision in their favor was made by a semi-judicial body, the Ontario Municipal Board, which is required by legislation to hear all sides of the issues it is concerned with and to make a fair decision based on the evidence it has before it.

In the city elections in December 1969 there were some changes, especially in the new Ward Seven which included many of the areas discussed in these articles. Oscar Sigsworth was the only sitting alderman who decided to run in the new Ward Seven; the two former aldermen for Don Vale, Regent Park and Trefann Court fled west and north to run in other wards. Mr. Sigsworth faced a number of candidates who would have been little different from him if they had been elected, one or two "reform" candidates who had no visible experience in city politics before the election, and two solid "reform" candidates, John Sewell and Karl Jaffary, who both had worked in the citizens' organizations in the ward. Jaffary was elected with 5400 votes; Sewell was elected with 5054 votes. Sigsworth was defeated, running well behind Sewell and Jaffary, with 3093. The only sitting school trustee to run in the new Ward Seven was Alan Archer, and he too was defeated badly. Elected were two "reform" candidates from middle-class backgrounds with strong campaign organizations; Noreen Gaudette, the candidate of the group of Trefann Court mothers, did not do well. These changes affected the quality of representation which the ward was able to get on municipal elected bodies. But the city-wide results were little different from those of other elections, and it is doubtful that in the same circumstances this new City Council and Board of Education would have acted any differently from the bodies which were making the political decisions in 1969.

The usual recourse of people who think that there is "something wrong" with city government is to argue that what is needed is "better people" elected to office. Instead of roofing contractors, insurance agents, and dumb lawyers, what is needed is architects, engineers, and smart lawyers. But close inspection of how city politics really works suggests that this position is social class snobbishness more than anything else. The architects, engineers and smart lawyers are almost always to be found doing the same old thing, a bit more smoothly, perhaps, but the same old thing.

A city council of Sewells would, certainly, be quite different from city councils anyone has ever known; but what would be different about it would be not the individual decisions it would make on specific issues, but rather the changes in the structure of city government and in the distribution of responsibility and power which it would make. It is possible to conceive of a reorganized city government where political power was returned to the citizens and their representatives remained representative and accountable. But it is extremely difficult even to imagine how such a reorganization might be brought about.

In the meanwhile, people are constantly finding themselves victimized by city government. When this happens not to an individual but to a group, and when the harm being done is extreme, some groups are prepared to take political action to protest and to try to force a change on city government. Usually, however, they undertake this kind of action knowing full well that it is virtually certain to prove useless. The people whose activities have been recorded here are realists; they knew all the time that they couldn't get anywhere at City Hall. They tried, nevertheless, partly perhaps because of a residual hope that this time things would be different, but largely because it was no longer possible for them to sit back and take what was happening to them with no protest whatsoever.

City politicians and bureaucrats are well aware of the threat posed to them by political organizations of people who have until now been completely unorganized and almost totally inactive in politics. They know that success by one or two citizens' organizations might destroy the "you can't fight City Hall" attitude and encourage other similar groups to spring up and to tackle city government on a host of other issues. So the politicians and bureaucrats are fighting back, and they are doing so very effectively. People are getting nowhere. What look like small but real successes turn out to be the prelude to complete failure. People find themselves back where they started from, and often worse off than they were. All their letters, protests, petitions, briefs, delegations, representations, meetings, demonstrations, and pickets produce nothing.